D0948838

Intelligent Buildings
Strategies for Technology and Architecture

Intelligent Buildings
Strategies for Technology and Architecture

by
Michelle D. Gouin and Thomas B. Cross

1986
Dow Jones-Irwin
Homewood, Illinois 60430

This publication is designed to provide accurate and
authoritative information in regard to the subject matter
covered. It is sold with the understanding that the
publisher is not engaged in rendering legal, accounting, or
other professional service. If legal advice or other expert
assistance is required, the services of a competent
professional person should be sought.

*From a Declaration of Principles jointly adopted by a Committee
of the American Bar Association and a Committee of Publishers.*

ISBN 0-87094-667-6
Library of Congress Catalog Card No. 85-72718

Printed in the United States of America

1 2 3 4 5 6 7 8 9 0 KP 3 2 1 0 9 8 7 6

This book is meant primarily for tenants and developers, although architects can use it to gain an understanding of which buildings are best suited to integrate information technology. Geared as it is to those who invest in them, either by building them or residing in them, this book presents the topic in the light of intelligent buildings as business tools. They are business tools by virtue of the information technology integral to their structure, which gives their owners and their tenants capabilities beyond that enjoyed in traditional buildings.

In order to use this tool, the "what" of intelligent buildings must be understood. What are they? What do they do? What services do they offer? What systems make these service offerings possible? What effects do their systems have on buildings and people? And, finally, what implications does information technology have for future building design? Each of these questions requires at least one chapter to answer, and some require more.

The first question is answered in Chapter One: What Is an Intelligent Building? It contrasts intelligent buildings with traditional buildings, explains briefly which information systems are responsible for the contrast, and takes the reader through a guided tour of an intelligent building. Chapter Two presents the business case, the "why" of intelligent buildings: the driving forces behind their emergence and the benefits they provide both developers and tenants. These benefits are part of what intelligent buildings do.

Chapters Three and Four present the services that intelligent building tenants can enjoy, if they choose. Chapter Three looks at office automation in an intelligent building. Chapter Four presents the concept of a central building information center, which negates the need for each tenant buying all of their automated office equipment. The building information center provides equipment and services to tenants on a rented, leased, or as-used basis. It may also sell office automation equipment.

Chapter Five presents the systems which support office information services. Chapter Six presents automated building-control systems, or information technology applied to the running of the building itself. Office information systems and building systems have traditionally been two separate fields. However, with recent advances in technology, both have become dependent on computer support. Chapter Seven describes the integration of the systems discussed independently in Chapters Five and Six into an intelligent building information systems (IBIS). This integration is made possible by the merging of the two technologies into one.

Chapter Eight views the impact of introducing technology into the office building environment. How does it affect the building? How does it affect the people in the building? What are some of the steps that can be taken to counteract negative effects? Chapter Nine goes further by describing how buildings themselves can best be designed to integrate information technology to meet the needs of their tenants. Intelligent buildings must be able to attract tenants by providing comfortable and productive environments. Both tenants and developers benefit when intelligent buildings are intelligently designed.

Michelle D. Gouin

CONTENTS

and Dust. Negative Impact of Information Technology on People: *Space. Changed Lighting Needs. Acoustics. Paper.* The Role of Furniture. Information Technology and New Organizational Space Needs: *Space Planning. What Does This Mean for Space Allocation?*

CHAPTER ONE

The best definition of an intelligent building is one that is fully leased.

What Is an Intelligent Building?

INTRODUCTION

What is an intelligent building? The answer involves many aspects of buildings, their purpose and design among them. This chapter explains the following:

- How an intelligent building differs from a "dumb" building.
- What systems make intelligent buildings "smart."
- What it is like to tour an intelligent building.

BUILDINGS IN GENERAL VERSUS INTELLIGENT BUILDINGS

People generally take buildings for granted without having a clear idea of their purpose and functions. What is a building? On the simplest level, it is a structure that encloses space. It consists of floors, walls, and a roof. Its primary purpose is to shelter people, although most buildings also provide occupants with heating, air-conditioning, and other amenities. A building's design determines how it does so.

Interior building design encourages or discourages certain types of occupant activities. It constrains or facilitates communications or information flow, and it encourages or hinders occupants' interaction. Interaction is increasingly important in a business world dependent on information. How do people exchange information? And how is that information used in being productive? Building design, in effect, influences productivity.

A building is also a structure which serves the people inside it while they are working. When a building has a positive influence on productivity, it is intelligently designed. When it serves the needs of the "information age" business community, it is an intelligent building (see Figure 1-1).

A myriad of information technology is integrated in the intelligent building structure: telecommunications, data communications, and building automation equipment. This supports the most advanced telephone models, computers, satellite dishes, and television systems—all of which provide efficient building management tools for owners and sophisticated electronic communications tools for tenants (see Figure 1-2).

Intelligent buildings combine two previously separate sets of technologies through an information network. They are the building management technologies (building automation), . . .

FIGURE 1-1

Cityplace, in Hartford, Connecticut, has been called "the world's first intelligent building."

SOURCE: United Technologies Building Systems Company

FIGURE 1–2

Voice and data are transmitted simultaneously through an advanced telecommunications system which is offered to tenants of "intelligent buildings." Through the phone, business tenants can "plug into" a variety of services, including word and data processing, electronic mail and filing, satellite transmission and other office automation services.

SOURCE: United Technologies Building Systems Company

control such systems as heating and air conditioning, and the information technologies (office automation), which control communications operations. Together they are the "high tech" side of intelligent buildings.

How do buildings incorporate high tech equipment and still provide a comfortable environment for their occupants? This is an important issue because information technology can negatively affect the work environment and the people in it if there are temperature changes and increased noise levels. Again, the answer is design—building design is responsible for the work environment. This is the "high touch" side of intelligent buildings. An intelligently designed building not only provides an appropriate environment, but incorporates the information equipment, which businesses increasingly demand, in a manner that best serves its occupants. Since this involves the comfortable interface of man and machine, an intelligent building is also "ergonomically" designed.

Its information network incorporates the equipment for all types of communications, making interactions as swift and easy as possible, encouraging innovation, and promoting productivity. Since it brings people together, the intelligent building is people-oriented and reflects the philosophy of organizations that realize people are the most expensive and the most important components of modern business.

In sum, an intelligent building provides more than an attractive roof over tenants' heads. It is, ultimately, a business tool to both its owners and its tenants (see Table 1-1).

A building may incorporate various types of technology and therefore be intelligent to various degrees. A truly intelligent building is one that incorporates most, if not all, of the systems and design features covered in this book. In the future, we would expect it to be compatible with even more advanced technology.

TABLE 1-1 A "Dumb" Building Versus a "Smart" Building

A "Smart Building:	A "Dumb" Building:
• Encloses space and also provides the "high tech" information network that supports "high tech" office and building automation.	• Is a structure that encloses space. It consists of floors, walls, and a roof.
• Shelters and supports the people inside it. It is "high touch."	• Provides shelter for people.
• Has individually programmable building systems for customized personal environments.	• May have air conditioning and other building systems.
• Encourages productivity and innovation in its occupants through design.	• Influences activities through its design.
• Facilitates information flow and encourages positive patterns of interaction.	• Constrains or facilitates movement and encourages or hinders patterns of interaction.
• Is an important business tool for builders and occupants alike.	• Can be a financial millstone around an organization's neck.

FIGURE 1–3

A shot of the front of 550 Madison Avenue, the new AT&T Headquarters, located in New York City.

Only such a building can realize the benefits of interconnection and integration of its separate systems within an integrated whole (see Figure 1–3).

THE ANATOMY OF AN INTELLIGENT BUILDING

How are intelligent buildings different from traditional "dumb" buildings? How are they communicators and facilitators? And how do they function as important business tools for both developers and tenants? The answers lie in the information systems they contain, and the integration of these systems into one intelligent building information network. Traditional buildings generally are not equipped in this way.

What are these information systems? Relating them to parts of the human body helps in understanding their technology:

- Heart: This is the telecommunications system which supplies the lifeblood—the communications system—to the tenants of an intelligent building. It provides both the telephones, and more importantly, the central switching equipment through which all building telephones are connected; it also provides the building's telecommunications link to the outside world. Without these systems, a building will not attract tenants today or in the future.
- Eyes and Ears: These are the systems which continually guard tenant safety. Intelligent buildings have electronic "eyes and ears" which sense minute—possibly life threatening—changes in the building environment. Unauthorized intrusions, the outbreak of fire, and other environmental problems are quickly detected. The proper alarms and measures are then taken by these security and life-support systems to protect the building and its occupants.
- Regulatory System: This is the comfort system. It continually monitors the environment and makes subtle adjustments in air quality, temperature, and lighting, and so forth. It is called the Energy Management and Control System, or EMCS, and keeps the intelligent building environment functioning smoothly.
- Nervous System: This is the wiring that links all building systems together (see Figure 1–4). The heart, the eyes and ears, the regulatory system, all the information equipment

FIGURE 1–4

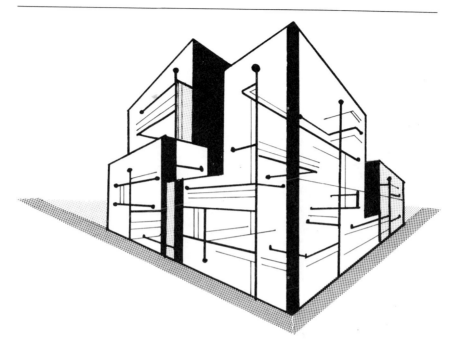

A "smart" building has a nervous system which connects every point to every other point.

and services offered through an intelligent building are supported by the building's nervous system. This system is called a local area network, or LAN.

- Brain: The interconnection or integration of these systems within one intelligent building information network requires a central point for network management. This can be called the Command and Control Center. Here, messages regarding the status of the building's systems are received, instructions are given, and overall intelligent building information systems are managed.
- Lungs: In the human body, lungs provide clean air. In the intelligent building, systems called uninterrupted power systems (UPS) and power conditioners, function as lungs to assure a clean supply of power. Without them, the rest of the system would suffer failure or loss of information.

What does a building with these basic information systems "look" like? How does it work? A guided tour provides the answers, and highlights many of the systems and services discussed in later chapters.

A GUIDED TOUR THROUGH AN INTELLIGENT BUILDING

What do you see when you look at an intelligent building? You might see a shiny new skyscraper (see Figure 1–5), or you might see a graceful old building (see Figure 1–6). The outside appearance will not tell you that it is an intelligent building unless you spot a satellite dish on top. It is what is *inside* a building that makes it intelligent.

Walk inside. The first thing you encounter is an electronic tenant directory terminal in the lobby, complete with a set of easy-to-follow instructions. It guides you through a list of tenants, their businesses and locations in the building, and even their schedules.

FIGURE 1–5

Main Street Centre, a $150 million twin office complex under construction in Richmond, VA, is one of a new generation of intelligent buildings.

SOURCE: United Technologies Building Systems Company

FIGURE 1-6

The Curtis Center, in Philadelphia, built in 1911 and listed in the National Register of Historic Places, is believed to be the largest historic office renovation in the country.

SOURCE: United Technologies Building Systems Company

It gives you a wealth of information, which can be updated quickly and easily. An electronic tenant directory is dynamic not static, responding to changes in tenants needs.

Stroll through the building. Let's say you have an appointment with Rudy Munguia, the vice president of Intelligent Building Corporation (IBC). IBC is in Suite 2804. Miracle of miracles, there is an elevator waiting at the lobby level! You don't know it, but an elevator is waiting because elevators in this intelligent building are programmed so that an idle one always returns to the lobby level.

Step inside the elevator and push the button for the 28th

FIGURE 1–7

The LTV Center in Dallas features "talking" elevators. It is also equipped with state-of-the-art communications systems for tenants to share.

SOURCE: United Technologies Building Systems Company

floor. A voice calls out floor numbers, so that you don't have to crane your neck for 28 floors watching numbers light up on an overhead panel (see Figure 1–7).

Follow your customized map, the one the tenant directory gave you. No longer do you have to wander around; you know where you are going. There's IBC, and you are on time for your appointment.

You check in with the secretary . . . some things never change! Rudy is still driving to work through early morning rush-hour traffic to meet you, but he has called his secretary on his cellular telephone to let her know that he is running late. While waiting, you take the time to notice the spaciousness of the reception area and talk with the secretary about your first experience with intelligent buildings. "Electronic directories and talking elevators!" you say. "What next?"

Rudy walks in and inadvertently answers your question. As he escorts you into his office, the light goes on. "Who turned on the lights?" you ask Rudy. "Nobody did. And if I leave the room for more than 12 minutes, the lights turn off automatically. Since I always forget to turn out lights, this system keeps my utility bills down."

Rudy tells you more about intelligent buildings. Not only are the lights in his office controlled automatically, but airflow and temperature are also monitored and adjusted in each office (see Figure 1–8). Although this means energy and cost savings, Rudy

FIGURE 1–8

Lights, heating and air-conditioning are controlled automatically to make this a comfortable building.

is actually more interested in his own comfort. He has programmed the office sensors for the very warm environment he likes, even though his personal computer isn't too wild about it.

You are shocked and ask him, '"Don't computers need very low temperatures? Don't they need to be coddled (even at the expense of their users)?" Rudy tells you that would be the case if very sensitive equipment were located in his office. However, this intelligent building "knows" Rudy's IBM–AT can take a little extra dust, lower humidity, and higher temperatures than mainframe computers. Thus in Rudy's office, his comfort has priority. It doesn't make sense to have the entire building environment controlled by the needs of particularly sensitive equipment which can be located in rooms that are designed especially for them.

You notice just how comfortable his office is and that there are lots of windows. Rudy tells you that the whole building is "ergonomically designed," or designed so that people's needs and machine needs don't conflict. People want windows, and windows

---

FIGURE 1–9

Your office is a jungle of wires: Rudy's isn't. In his office, Rudy can move his workstation anywhere he wants, and easily move all its supporting devices (electrical, computer, telephone, etc.).

cause problems for machines. Therefore, he explains, we design buildings so that special machine rooms are located in the center of the building, and tenants' offices are around the perimeter.

You wish your office looked like his (see Figure 1-9). His is expansive and uncluttered. Your office is a jungle of wires and cables. Where does he plug in his telephones, personal computers, coffee pots, and printers? Rudy tells you that the flexible wiring systems of the intelligent building hide all those cables. His personal computer, for example, is plugged into the hidden wiring systems, and there's no extension cord in sight. Wiring is also hidden by his desk which is designed to meet the lighting and wiring needs of information equipment.

Rudy exclaims, "I forgot to check for mail!" "Doesn't the secretary simply bring it in," you ask. No, Rudy has voice mail that is tied into the building's answering service. How does he know if anyone has tried to reach him while he was out? The message lamp on his telephone is lit. Why couldn't his secretary have taken the message? Either he or she was also out of the office, or someone wanted to leave a message in their own words and in their own voice. The caller knew Rudy would hear exactly what was said, the way it was meant, and the danger of misinterpretation would be minimized. Rudy hears his message and is not required to speak with the client who sent it. He sends an acknowledgment and handles his client's request.

Rudy needs to send a signed document to his client. He can use the old "snail mail" postal service, which would take three days to deliver, but this is an emergency. A contract for a major building project is on the line, so Rudy uses an alternative—a' facsimile system. With this type of system he can send a picture of the document in 15 seconds if his client also has a telecopier (facsimile) machine to receive it. But these machines are extremely expensive, much too expensive for Rudy and his client to cost-justify for relatively infrequent use.

Rudy is lucky. Both he and his client have offices in intelligent buildings which provide both information systems and services to their tenants. This is done on a shared basis through an information center (see Figure 1-10). Rudy calls it the building's "general store." He's used the fax before, so he knows that he only needs to call the general store and reserve a time slot (As soon as one is available, please). No one is scheduled for the next half hour, so Rudy invites you to go with him and see another intelligent building feature.

FIGURE 1-10

1800 Kennedy Boulevard, in Philadelphia, offers tenants shared information services, including telecommunications, information management, and office automations, through a Resource Center located on the second floor.

SOURCE: United Technologies Building Systems Company

At the building's information center, Rudy sends his document. He will be billed on a per-page basis, and he can either pay immediately or have the charge added to his monthly statement. All of the intelligent building services he uses are billed to him on a single monthly statement through this same center. It is also the place that controls all equipment systems and services. You ask Rudy to show you the listing of services available to tenants. These range from "PCs to pencils," Rudy says, "and much more." The center demonstrates, trains in the use of, sells, and maintains personal computers and other equipment. You are amazed at all the services an intelligent building provides its tenants. "It all boils down to: What do you need?" Rudy explains.

Rudy's pager is beeping. He reaches for a handy telephone and calls his secretary to find out who is paging him. One of Rudy's employees, Andrew McKay, is trying to get in touch with him.

You and Rudy return to Rudy's office. As you do so, you notice the spaciousness of the building, its wide hallways, the appealing decor, and what appear to be a number of lounges and cafeterias. You remark to Rudy on their attractiveness and their varying styles. Yes, this is all part of the "high touch" side of an intelligent building, he explains. Certainly, by this time you understand the "high tech" aspect of intelligent buildings. But what is "high touch"?

High touch is the person-oriented side of intelligent buildings, designed in response to the sense of isolation some people develop while working with personal computers. "After sitting, staring at my monitor all morning, I like to get away from all that equipment," Rudy says. "There's a terminal in every room in my office. But I don't want to be too far away. I want to stay in the building. So I visit my favorite cafeteria, the one with all the windows and plants, and grab a bite to eat. Or I go to a lounge, sink into a comfortable chair, have a cup of coffee, and relax.

You see the possibilities. This is a way to meet fellow business people in a comfortable environment. Yes, Rudy tells you, he met his accountant in one of the building lounges. The accountant is on the fifth floor, and Rudy sends him his financial data electronically. How is this done? Over the building's information network. Information can be sent from any one point in the building to any other. That's how the telephones, computers, energy sensors, and so forth function. Telephones, too? Does this mean Rudy can use the same network to get outside the building? Definitely.

Rudy regularly uses his personal computer (PC) to tie into the building network and reach data bases or on-line information services outside. In this way he can check his PC screen to find out quickly and easily what his stock is worth. And his information is current, within the last quote. You have an image of the whole building plugged into a vast information network which includes other buildings and even private homes (see Figure 1-11). Rudy also uses this network to confer electronically with Andrew McKay, the person paging him.

FIGURE 1-11 Image of Buildings Plugged into Each Other

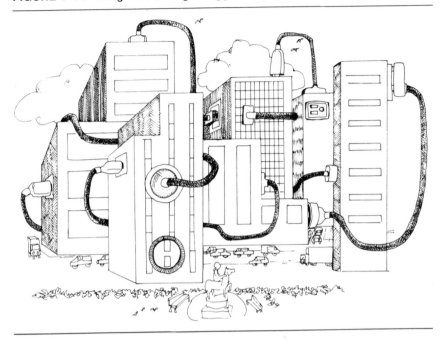

Andrew is a telecommuter who writes specialized software programs for the company. He has a mailbox at IBC and comes to office lounge parties, but he works at home. As a self-motivated person who needs little direction and enjoys extremely flexible hours, he is the ideal telecommuter. He does, however, like to keep in touch with Rudy. They schedule meetings once a week to talk over projects, but Andrew also calls when he needs to brainstorm with Rudy. This time, Andrew needed Rudy to look over some of his work for input. Rudy brings a copy of it up on his screen and they go over the program together, speaking over the telephone. After making some changes to smooth out rough spots, Andrew signs off.

You wonder what else is behind those intelligent building walls. Andrew's ability to "travel" the communication network makes him as accessible as if he were actually in the building. When you express surprise, Rudy responds: "Oh, that's nothing! Come to the teleconference we have scheduled in a few minutes." As with facsimile service, he has reserved the teleconferencing

FIGURE 1-12   Levels of Linkage

Traditional office: terminals do not communicate with each other.

Equipment linked within the office: messages can be sent from one terminal to another within each office.

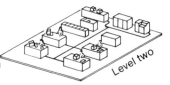

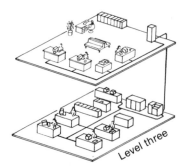

Offices networked within the building: individuals can send messages from one office to another in an intelligent building.

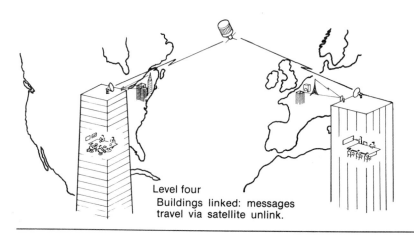

Level four
Buildings linked: messages travel via satellite unlink.

room and full-motion video equipment for this purpose. Having only heard of this form of communication, you're eager to evaluate it. Is it really like "being there?"

It is. When the teleconference starts, you have the feeling that you are really with the people on the screen. Their room and your room are now one. You could be in Denver or Houston. They could be in Tokyo or London. With video teleconferencing, you are all in the same place (see Figure 1–12).

CHAPTER TWO

Smart buildings: practical, affordable, necessary.
Anthony Autorino
Chairman and CEO
Building Systems Company
United Technologies

The Business Case
for Intelligent Buildings

INTRODUCTION

"Smart" buildings are an improvement over traditional "dumb" buildings by virtue of the information technology inherent in their structure. How much of an enhancement are intelligent buildings? Enough to justify the cost of integrating information systems into buildings? While the integration of information systems into a building's design in the initial phases of construction is less expensive than retrofitting an existing building, both are costly alternatives for builders. Tenants who want to use intelligent building information services also need to invest time and/or money by renting or purchasing automated office equipment. Do the benefits of building or renting in an intelligent building outweigh the costs?

Organizations rent offices in intelligent buildings to simplify the installation or use of office automation equipment and to boost productivity. Increased productivity means a small or medium-sized company can compete with larger companies that have their own information networks.

Intelligent buildings are a good investment for developers. They attract the increasingly sophisticated tenants who demand both information technology and the environment in which to use it comfortably. Their automated building technology also makes the running of this environment more cost-effective and manageable.

These reasons for organization and developer interest in intelligent buildings raise the following questions, however:

- In what ways are intelligent buildings productive buildings?
- How does office automation affect productivity?
- How is an intelligent building a good investment for the developer?

THE MARKETPLACE AND OTHER DRIVING FORCES BEHIND THE EMERGENCE OF INTELLIGENT BUILDINGS

The answer to the above questions lies in today's marketplace and evolving information technology. Information technology makes the emergence of intelligent buildings possible. To a large extent, it also creates the marketplace forces which demand rapid and easy communications. The following modern marketplace conditions have lead to the emergence of intelligent buildings:

- Ours is an "information economy." Today's main business is information or knowledge production.
- Businesses must increase office productivity to remain competitive.
- Office automation increases office productivity.
- Intelligent buildings facilitate office automation.
- Management and operational costs of running buildings are increasing.
- Regulatory change is opening new opportunities for telecommunications services in intelligent buildings.

The "Information Society" Economy

John Naisbitt's book, *Megatrends*, examines 10 critical trends in America. He considers the most subtle yet most important one to be the shift from an industrial to an information society.[1] Naisbitt cites the years 1956 and 1957 as the beginning of that trend.

In 1956, white-collar workers in technical, managerial, and clerical positions outnumbered blue-collar workers for the first time in American history. White-collar workers produce information rather than goods, so that "[a]lthough we continue to think we live in an industrial society, we have in fact changed to an economy based on the creation and distribution of information," Naisbitt says.[2]

In 1957, the Russians launched Sputnik, introducing the era of global satellite communications. Naisbitt believes that satellites, especially those launched by American shuttles, are an important part of the coming transformation of the earth into a global village. The creation of a global village through instantaneous communications between any two points on earth means that technology virtually eliminates distance.

A large number of white-collar workers are now concerned with the production of information. Their use of sophisticated devices to communicate this information quickly and easily has led to an economy largely dependent on the mass production of information. To ignore this basic shift from an "industrial economy" to an "information economy" is to risk the health of businesses functioning in it. The emergence of intelligent buildings is a major response to the needs of smaller organizations operating in this economy.

Businesses Must Increase Office Productivity

In today's competitive business climate, "productivity" is the rallying cry as office costs increase at a rate of 15 percent a year.[3] This increase is due in part to the large growth in the number of knowledge workers and the corresponding low growth of office productivity (as compared to farm and factory productivity increases). According to one study, the productivity of office workers has increased by only 4 percent in the 1974 to 1984 period, while the productivity of factory workers increased by 100 percent. Farm worker productivity went up by 200 percent in the same 10-year period.[4]

Roughly 53 percent of the adult workforce in this country is engaged in white-collar work, accounting for 70 percent of the total industry payroll.[5] An economy dependent on services produced by a large, highly paid group of office workers cannot grow in the face of rapidly increasing office costs and low productivity gains. This gap must be bridged in order to maintain a healthy "information economy."

Office Automation (OA) Increases Office Productivity

What tools are available for the production of information? Office automation (OA) equipment is one means of increasing office productivity. This, of course, produces higher profits—the goal of all businesses. The automated office machines that manage information best are today's most valuable tools. They include telephones, integrated workstations, telecopiers and facsimile, word/text/data processors, and personal computers. These devices allow office workers to communicate with each other by electronic and voice mail, and gain access to on-line computer data bases.

Judiciously selected and implemented, such equipment increases both clerical productivity and management effectiveness in most office environments. It also increases people's efficiency since they are largely relieved of tedious. time-consuming tasks like typing, filing, copying, mailing, and sorting. Furthermore, it helps people reduce time wasted on fruitless activities. For example, a study showed that 25 percent of knowledge workers' time is spent in waiting for meetings to start and in making travel ar-

FIGURE 2-1 Time Wasted

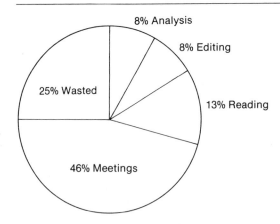

The consulting firm of Booz, Allen and Hamilton compiled results from a study of 15 corporations regarding workday activities. One quarter of key workers' time—from salesmen to vice presidents—was wasted on activities such as waiting for meetings to start and making travel arrangements.

SOURCE: Daniel Goleman, "The Electronic Rorschach," *Psychology Today*, Feb. 1983, p. 39.

rangements (see Figure 2–1). OA can save an average of 14 percent of this time if activities are carefully planned and implemented.[6] In addition, "many jobs are so unexciting that they deserve to be replaced by machines to release people for more creative endeavors," as office automation specialist James H. Green notes.[7]

The information services which office automation provides workers helps them access information and decrease information "float." Information float is the time that information spends in transit from its point of origination to its final destination. Quicker access to information and a reduction in information float can allow people to act rapidly and make timely decisions. In the long run, the benefit is a corporation's increased competitiveness and business survival.

Intelligent Buildings Facilitate Office Automation

Communication is the byword of the Information Age, and the major function of intelligent buildings is to offer its occupants the ability to communicate quickly using voice, data, and image transmissions. Communications in the intelligent building travel person-to-person, person-to-machine, person-to-terminal, and terminal-to-terminal. The intelligent building not only incorporates the myriad of devices necessary for these divergent forms of communications, but also links them together through an in-place intelligent building information network.

Integration is the all-important feature of both intelligent buildings and fully automated offices. The fully automated office information system is a comprehensive, integrated system in which all devices work together. This networking of information equipment provides the multitude of OA services—such as electronic mail—which workers use to access needed information. Intelligent buildings extend the office facilities throughout the entire building and to the public or private networks beyond. According to John Daly, Corporate Telecommunications Manager for the Planning & Research Corp., "Office automation and intelligent buildings go hand in hand. Electronic enhancement of the building is the mechanism by which office automation is really accomplished."[8]

Because information tools attract highly skilled employees that businesses increasingly need, the quality of the overall work environment is becoming critical to employees. As the competition for staff that is familiar with new office technology increases (it is currently in short supply in many areas), an important criterion in a prospective employee's job search is the type of business "power tools" available to them. The intelligent building is equipped to provide both the power tools demanded by highly skilled employees and the environment in which to use them productively.

Energy and Management Costs of Running Buildings are Increasing

Building owners facing rising energy costs stress their need to reduce operating costs and manage building facilities (air, space, energy) more efficiently. Building automation systems, such as energy management and control systems (EMCS), present an effective method of meeting these needs.

The building's information technology network not only serves management functions of energy control, fire management, life safety, and security, but also the voice and data needs of a building's tenants. An information network that supports building and office automation systems allows for the benefits of centralized management and control of all building and office systems, while reducing the networking costs of what were previously two separately wired systems. Through an information network system, designers of intelligent buildings bring already existing technologies together in cost-effective ways.

Regulatory Change is Opening New Opportunities for Telecommunications Services in Intelligent Buildings

The telecommunications industry's new post-divestiture competitive environment is opening new opportunities for sharing telecommunications services. The Bell System no longer supplies all business telecommunications needs. While the Bell operating companies still provide local telephone service, and some sell equipment through separate subsidiaries, many essential communications functions provided prior to divestiture may no longer be available. These essential functions include: system management, maintenance, equipment leasing, equipment service, and long-distance service. This means that, at the very least, building owners must provide their own wiring systems. They must also make choices among the above essential communication functions in order to obtain telecommunications services for tenants. Hence, the building owner may have no choice but to be in the phone service business if he or she wants to keep tenants and attract new ones.

AN INTELLIGENT BUILDING IS A BUSINESS TOOL

Intelligent buildings, in general, are not the financial millstones that dumb buildings can be. They are a financial resource to both owners and tenants because they are—thanks to their information systems—business tools. Like all business tools, they offer many benefits to their users, both tenants and developers.

Benefits to Tenants

Among the many benefits that intelligent buildings offer tenants are:

- Shared tenant services—How you get it
- Shared information services—What you get
- "One-stop" shopping—Where you get it
- Comfortable office environment—Where you use it

Shared tenant services. Multitenant intelligent buildings attempt to provide the small or medium-sized company with the same information tools that larger companies enjoy. One building-wide system is installed by the building owner and remarketed to the tenants, rather than all the tenants of a large office building buying separate communications systems. "Shared tenant services" (STS) has become a synonym for the multitenant intelligent building. Lew Malouf, of Intecom, defines STS as, "the sharing of equipment, facilities, and other resources among many distinct and individual businesses in a multitenant environment."[9]

Whereas tenants can provide their own information services, information systems represent costly investments which many small and medium-sized companies are not willing or able to make. Only by sharing can these businesses enjoy the benefits of information technology. By sharing equipment with other tenants and by leasing only those services required on a monthly basis from a central building office, small to medium-sized tenants have access to sophisticated services previously unobtainable. As business competition increases, telecommunications services to small and medium-sized companies may mean the difference between survival or failure. A multitenant intelligent building therefore provides office communications capabilities to companies that cannot afford them, but cannot afford to do without them.

Shared information services. The services offered to tenants on a shared basis include:

- Sale, rent, and/or lease of a variety of information equipment.
- Word and text processing support.
- Message center.
- Shared video teleconferencing.
- Data base time-sharing.
- Tenant/Text—Tenant directory listings.
- Modem pooling.
- Automatic routing of long-distance calls to least cost carriers.
- Shared long-distance.
- Encryption—systems security.
- Archival storage.
- Tenant services training.

Information service offerings such as centralized word processing, photocopying, facsimile, telex, printing, and telephone answering services can be made available at rates far lower than individual systems can offer. Similarly, expensive advanced services such as message centers and video teleconferencing become cost-effective in multitenant buildings (see Chapters 3 and 4 for discussion on these services). These services are made possible in intelligent buildings by state-of-the-art, third generation software driven systems. They are more technically advanced than small systems that tenants are likely to purchase individually.

The intelligent building also provides its user access to intelligent resources such as:

- Building concierge.
- Conference and "war rooms" that can be reserved.
- Temporary services, e.g., leased staff.
- Consulting services.
- Package, mailroom, courier, and delivery services.
- Travel, conference, and meeting-planning services.
- Day care and health/recreational gyms.

- Office supplies/services.
- Computer-aided design services.
- Educational and training services.

One-stop shopping. The multitenant building offers shared tenant services as the single point of contact between tenants and the local telephone company, long-distance carriers, and installation and maintenance services. Physically, this point of contact can be a building information center (BIC), which provides tenants with information technology and services on a rented, leased, purchased, or as-used basis. The primary aim of such a center is to support all tenant needs from a single source.

Tenants of an intelligent building avoid becoming individual small telephone companies, while obtaining state-of-the-art equipment and services. Hence, they avoid the agonies of choice among multitudes of systems, the burden of large capital outlays, and the ordeal of systems maintenance. Such side benefits as the elimination of equipment-room costs and simplified billing procedures are also available to tenants. The following points illustrate these benefits:

- *No need to make complex decisions regarding choice of information systems.* Choosing communications systems has become a complex and confusing process following the divestiture of AT&T, and one that many are happy to forgo. Since January 1, 1984, the date the divestiture of AT&T went into effect, there has been no Bell System to benignly guide the business community in its choice, installation, and maintenance of information technology. Instead, a host of new vendors has appeared, each loudly proclaiming the outstanding points of his or her systems. Lacking the technical expertise necessary to evaluate these systems, the business community has reacted with confusion and dismay, often turning a blind eye to the benefits of this technology.

    When information technology is supplied to tenants through a building's information center, it is no longer necessary to run the gauntlet of equipment suppliers to obtain a working system. The system is provided for them, *de facto*, and the only decision remaining is . . . "to rent or not to rent."
- *No capital outlay for a new phone system.* Individual tenants never need to be concerned with equipment purchases, installation, maintenance, services, or staff.

- *Eliminate management and administrative costs.* Personnel normally needed for order tracking, optimizing long-distance traffic, or providing technical support are supplied through the building center. Tenants do not have to find these specialists or salary them.

    Systems that are provided by the building owner and backed up by a maintenance staff allow tenants to feel secure in the knowledge that not only are they served by the most advanced systems, but that those systems will not "go down," or fail.

- *Ongoing, on-site operations.* Intelligent building managers offer tenants a private telecommunications department. Service technicians are on-site, reducing costs for moves and changes and for routine maintenance. Tenants can also obtain training, consultation, and routine services.

- *Eliminate equipment-room costs.* The need to purchase and support special environments, power requirements, and flooring is eliminated. Fire codes and insurance issues are also eliminated.

- *Detailed service bills.* Each tenant receives a single, detailed bill for all building services used. An important component is the detailed telephone call-accounting reports which provide tenants with more information on calling patterns than a small, unsophisticated accounting system purchased separately could provide.

- *Growth capabilities.* In essence, each tenant has his or her own individual system within the larger building network. A small tenant is better able to grow within a large system than on his or her own. When tenants do need extra capacity, they can get this from the central service "one-stop" shopping area.

Not only is shared tenant service more affordable, "but it can save tenants a lot of aggravation. It can be chaotic for a company to select a communications system that's right for them. We do it all, from selection to maintenance," said David Leninger, chairman of Multinet Communications Corporation (MCC) of Dallas.[10]

A comfortable office environment. John Naisbitt expresses the notion of high tech/high touch when he says, "We are moving in the dual direction of high tech/high touch, matching each new technology with a compensatory human response."[11] "High touch" refers to the need for a rehumanization of the office, as increasing amounts of high technology are introduced. There will be a greater need for human contact and "workstation personalization" in the future office. This is because the composition of the work force is changing, worker expectations are different, work ethics have changed, and the activities performed by this new work force are more demanding.

Changing work force composition. The composition of the work force is evolving from the traditional pyramid organizational structure dominated by clerical workers, to a diamond-shaped structure that emphasizes the growing numbers of knowledge workers (see Figure 2-2). Concern with high touch environments is due to the greater number of knowledge workers—the managers and professionals considered to be the key to increased office productivity and organizational effectiveness. Their experiences and expectations concerning the quality of the office environment differ significantly from those of clerical personnel.

FIGURE 2-2 Changing Work force Composition

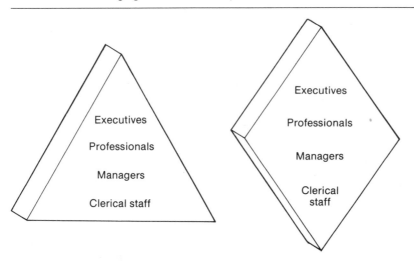

The overall shape of the organization is shifting from a traditional pyramid structure to a diamond-shaped structure dominated by "knowledge" workers.

SOURCE: Daniel Goleman, "The Electronic Rorschach," *Psychology Today*, Feb. 1983, p. 43.

Changing worker expectations. Knowledge workers tend to be more vocal concerning working conditions. Results of a study conducted by the Center for Building Technology show that:

> Office design is an important factor in determining whether office automation succeeds or fails to increase organizational productivity and effectiveness. Research findings suggest that the employees of automated offices are more likely to place a high priority on the quality of the workplace than their counterparts working in traditional offices.[12]

Changing work ethics. A change in work ethics, combined with demands for higher-quality office environments, aggravates the problem of information technology discomforts. According to Leon O. Gouin, executive vice president of overseas exploration, AMAX Exploration, the work ethic in America has "gone down the tubes." Mr. George T. Trayer, a vice president of the Central Bank of Denver, claims these attitudes have an impact on the general work environment:

> John and Sally are not going to work where they are not happy and content because they are less than certain they want to work anyway. They are not going to sit in a chair that's uncomfortable at a table or desk that's too high or low, looking at a screen on a CRT with poor resolution, squinting through light glare while breathing cigarette smoke in air that feels like a sauna, go home take a couple of aspirin and come back tomorrow because of a work ethic that disappeared some years ago.[13]

In a recent survey of Fortune 500 chief executive officers (CEOs) by the American Society of Interior Designers, 99% said they believed well-designed offices affect worker productivity. John Young, CEO of Hewlett-Packard, noted, "You can and should improve environment. Bad surroundings distract—if environment is bad, people will spend more time complaining than being productive."[14]

More demanding work. Differing expectations and work ethics are not the only reason buildings need to be designed more intelligently, however. The work that knowledge workers do demands a supportive environment. Planning and creative thinking are important activities, and people engaged in these activities are often disrupted by environmental intrusions. Disruptions by normal activity or by information technology demand office designs which meet workers' needs.

Information technology has created a whole new set of office worker needs. Design criteria and guidelines are ultimately concerned with meeting the needs of the individual office worker. The intrusion of information technology into all levels of the office, including the executive, calls for an environment capable of compensating for the impersonal and, at times, uncomfortable interaction of man and machine.

The advent of the microcomputer-based workstation has enabled many jobs to be performed autonomously, thereby isolating individual workers from the groups to which they are assigned and from the organization as a whole. Although a certain amount of isolation is desirable in certain activities, it can mean that people lose touch with co-workers. Thus, settings are needed for informal social interactions among colleagues whose work consists of manipulating information on computer monitors. Workers will appreciate chances for interaction, visual relief, and recreation, as more of their time is spent seated in front of terminals in what may be increasingly tight spaces. Leisure areas can provide a welcome change from isolated work on a monitor and a place for much-needed human interaction.

Many areas are involved in implementing information technology. They include architecture, interior design, ergonomics, management and organization, office systems, telecommunications, electrical systems, lighting, acoustics, data processing, and environmental psychology. Due to the involvement in office design of all these fields, the computer is transforming the workplace in an increasingly paradoxical manner. Instead of creating "information sweatshops" characterized by an industrial-line inhumanity of rows of desks with computers on them, workplaces are being designed to maximize comfort and minimize the visibility of information devices.

Benefits to Owners

Lew Malouf, of Intecom, cites three reasons to be in the shared tenant services (STS) business. These are to accrue profit, to provide needed services to others, and to differentiate one's property from others' in order to attract tenants.[15] Specifically, multi-tenant intelligent buildings provide their owners with:

- A marketing edge.

- Increased revenues.
- Improved facilities management.

Shared telecommunications attract tenants to a building, ensure that they will stay, defray corporate communications costs, and lower building costs by combining wiring, conduit, and space requirements.

Marketing edge. As tenants become increasingly sophisticated, demanding, and scarce, there is an intense competition among developers for them. Most cities have a three-year inventory of office space. According to an annual study of downtown office markets by Urban Investment & Development Co. of Chicago, more downtown office buildings have already been built in the mid-1980s than during all of the 1970s: 217.8 million square feet compared to 197.3 million square feet.[16] This office building boom has created a temporary glut in the market, producing intense competition among developers for tenants.

These tenants, in turn, are demanding more than walls, floors, and a roof. They are demanding comfortable spaces to work in and the information systems and services that intelligent buidings offer tenants on a shared basis. "Having shared service in your building doesn't mean an increase in rent. It *does* mean greater leasability," according to Philip Siler, of Olympia and York.[17]

The best definition of an intelligent building is one that is fully leased. Buildings that are not leased soon after construction are financial millstones around their owners' necks. "For every month a new building stands empty it costs the owner one percent of the total construction cost of that project," according to Joe Baker, of Northern Telecom.[18] Offering advanced equipment and services has become the latest method used to attract tenants.

In a recent author survey, 78 percent of the developers contacted said they had plans to build intelligent buildings that would include a mix of telephone, energy management, data processing, and teleconferencing systems, as well as secretarial services.[19] This is indicative of a trend toward use of information technologies as staple items.

Revenue generator. The prime motivator in any business venture is profit, and shared tenant services (STS) is no exception.

Table 2-1 Revenues Generated from Shared Tenant Services

Annual profit based on a per minute margin of: $1.20
Percent of tenant participation: 100.0%

	Number of Phones	CALL DURATION IN MIN/MONTH/PHONE			
		100	200	300	1,000
50,000	500	$60,000	$120,000	$180,000	$600,000
SQ. FT	250	$30,000	$60,000	$90,000	$300,000
	167	$20,040	$40,080	$60,120	$200,400
	67	$8,040	$16,080	$24,120	$80,400
100,000	1,000	$120,000	$240,000	$360,000	$1,200,000
SQ. FT.	500	$60,000	$120,000	$180,000	$600,000
	333	$39,960	$79,920	$119,880	$399,600
	67	$16,080	$32,160	$48,240	$160,800
200,000	2,000	$240,000	$480,000	$720,000	$2,400,000
SQ. FT.	1,000	$120,000	$240,000	$360,000	$1,200,000
	667	$80,040	$160,080	$240,120	$800,400
	267	$32,040	$64,080	$96,120	$320,400
300,000	3,000	$360,000	$720,000	$1,080,000	$3,600,000
SQ. FT.	1,500	$180,000	$360,000	$540,000	$1,800,000
	1,000	$120,000	$240,000	$360,000	$1,200,000
	400	$48,000	$96,000	$144,000	$480,000
500,000	5,000	$600,000	$1,200,000	$1,800,000	$6,000,000
SQ. FT.	2,500	$300,000	$600,000	$900,000	$3,000,000
	1,667	$200,040	$400,080	$600,120	$2,000,400
	667	$80,040	$160,080	$240,120	$800,400

SOURCE: Intelligent Buildings Corporation, Copyright 1985

Intelligent buildings used on a multitenant services basis provide profits for owners. It is estimated that building owners with a well-planned and well-operated building information system receive revenues as high as $25 per square foot per year, depending on the percent of tenant participation in shared services. Taking into account building size, this amount can be considerable (see Table 2–1). Developers can realize some savings and pass the rest on to tenants in the form of lower rents. Since this may attract tenants to the building, both the owner and tenant benefit.

Sources of revenue in the STS business include:

• Equipment sale, lease, or rent.
• Tenant and nontenant long-distance service.
• Equipment moves, adds, and changes.
• Sale of shared services.

More efficient and effective facilities management. Facilities management has to do with the efficient management of all building systems (air, lights, fire safety, security) and with energy-saving operations. Facilities management ensures that an intelligent building actually performs intelligently.

An intelligent building is managed centrally, automatically, with the most sophisticated electronic information equipment. Banks of monitors keep maintenance teams informed on the status of all systems. Some automated building systems have enough intelligence to let maintenance people know of problems, or even potential problems, that can be solved before the building environment is affected.

Although these systems are more complex than those found in dumb buildings, the same technologies provide the means and simplify facilities management through easy monitoring of all building automation systems. "You have a building that thinks for itself, in effect, making decisions that reduce maintenance, labor, and operating costs," according to Anthony B. Autorino.[20]

CHAPTER THREE

In the old days, it was said that three factors influenced office design—"location, location, location." A new formulation might be—"services, services, services."
Francis Duffy, Architect

The Services that an Intelligent Building Offers Tenants

OFFICE AUTOMATION SERVICES

System integration of intelligent buildings offers tenants virtually all the capabilities a modern office environment requires, such as:

- Telephones and the integrated workstation.
- Personal computing.
- Word and text processing.
- Voice mail.
- Electronic mail.
- Facsimile.
- On-line database access.
- Videotext.
- Teleconferencing capabilities.

Telephones and the Integrated Workstation

Increased competition in the phone market has brought a host of technological innovations, many of which apply to the computerized desk phone. Feature phones, for example, now offer single-button access to custom calling features such as call forwarding, speed dialing, bridging, and others that formerly required dialing a code to activate (see Figure 3–2).

Dramatically advanced integrated workstations comprise telephones and computer terminals, and these devices handle the

FIGURE 3-1

Photograph of the opened cabinets of the 3B20 simplex processors used for communications networking and office automation functionality in AT&T Headquarters at 550 Madison Avenue, New York City. The end cabinet, partially opened, is the ISN local area network.

FIGURE 3-2   The Meridian M3000 Touchphone

complete range of voice and data communications (see Figure 3-3.). They depend on digital transmission and switching, an enhancement of the basic way phones work that is analogous to the leap from mechanical adding machines to electronic calculators.

Personal Computers

The advent and proliferation of the personal computer (PC) as a multipurpose terminal has been key to the growth of data and telecommunications in business. In fact, it is considered to be the catalyst of office automation development.

While PCs have extensive applications, a key ingredient in the office environment is their ability to communicate with other office systems and equipment. Their full potential is largely unrealized when they stand alone. The combination of expensive peripherals and loss of information sharing results in lost office automation benefits. The local area network (LAN) is the primary

FIGURE 3-3 The Meridian M4020 Integrated Terminal

tool for overcoming this isolation. It provides a hardware/software network between computers, their peripherals, and host computers. Such a network allows the integration of PCs into a multiuser environment where they can:

- Access various databases.
- Produce graphics and design, do word processing, and transmit electronic and voice mail.
- Provide the equipment for certain forms of teleconferencing, such as computer conferencing.

Word and Text Processing

A word processor is a specialized computer for word processing and the sophisticated text preparation required for writing letters and documents. Word processing terminals and related storage devices can also be used for data storage and communications.

There is a trend in business toward decentralizing word processing by dispensing terminals to professionals and secretaries in different locations. Professionals gain more control over output this way, secretaries become more efficient, and faster document turnaround results. This, in turn, allows a reduction in, or at least a slower growth of, support staff.

Concurrent with decentralization is an increased need for communications among word processors. In multioffice environments, communications capability enables people to send documents rapidly from office to office, allows more input from key people, and permits rapid document preparation.

Communicating word processors require the same networking support as PCs in the multiuser environment. In an intelligent building, LANs can support both word processing and PC functions and allow both types of devices to communicate.

Voice Mail

Voice mail is essentially a sophisticated computerized answering machine that operates on a tone-generating telephone. It goes beyond telephone message-recording devices, however, by processing and communicating messages. This enhances the value of information throughout an organization and allows the user to:

- Record and store messages.
- Use stop, start, listen, and slow, normal, fast controls.
- Retrieve messages sequentially.

- Retrieve messages by random selection.
- Forward messages to individuals or groups.
- Distribute messages to lists stored in the system.
- Classify—such as "urgent" and "time-deliver."
- Customize information—such as traveling schedules.
- Secure confidential information.
- Use pause compression—for more concise messages.
- Access prompt and help functions stored in the system.

These functions help improve productivity and control telephone costs. They can be used to answer telephones with individual greetings on each extension, store the actual voice of the caller, activate and deactivate message-waiting indicators, and play the message back on command whenever and from wherever the called party wants to hear them.

The more sophisticated voice mail functions help:

- Control time spent recording and listening by touch-key control for stop, start, listen, slow, normal, and fast review.
- Identify and retrieve messages by individual names, time, and date.
- Classify messages—as "normal," "quick-ring" for immediate delivery during business hours, "urgent" for delivery after business hours, or as "time delivery."
- Categorize messages—as new (not yet heard), pending (awaiting action or reply), old (heard and stored in the system), and outbound.
- Provide quality voice reproduction, including retaining a speaker's expressions and inflections.
- Achieve a continuous natural flow of words (the system eliminates pauses throughout the recorded messages).
- Secure information with passwords—An individually created password permits access to specific information. A secretary's password, for example, might permit partial access to information and be used to ascertain who sent messages. A guest password could be given to vendors, family members, and others for leaving messages.
- Schedule and distribute messages by specified date and/or time.
- Decrease long-distance telephone costs by transmitting messages during lower-rate hours.
- Reduce employee hours spent on the telephone by reducing or eliminating the need for people to call back or transcribe messages.

- Record a variety of information in addition to messages, such as task progress reports and travel schedules, which can be quickly accessed and updated.
- Send and receive recorded messages.
- Store messages for either prompt or later retrieval or for longer periods.
- Send messages to individuals or groups.
- Transmit messages to distribution lists stored in the system.
- Append messages for re-routing.
- Confirm receipt of messages sent.

The advantages of voice mail are:

- It is a human and natural form of communication.
- The recipient can verify sender by voice recognition.
- It allows rapid and efficient message creation.
- It allows easy access through terminals and telephones.
- It allows rapid response to important messages.
- It includes emotional intent of messages.

Advantages of voice mail that accrue to management are:

- It increases management and staff productivity by improving the flow of information and eliminating "telephone tag."
- It provides prompt responses to requests from inside and outside the organization.
- It reduces telephone costs because messages are more concise and "party-not-available" call backs are eliminated.
- It saves time previously wasted by managers and staff failing to get through promptly.

The disadvantages of voice mail are:

- Note-taking is required by recipient.
- It is impossible to edit.
- It is difficult to document for record-keeping.
- It is impossible for lengthy communications.
- It can be difficult to annotate.
- Emphasis is lost when transcribed to written form.
- Expensive system overhead in transmission time and computer management is required.

Electronic Mail

Electronic mail can be used on many interactive devices that are supported by the intelligent building network. It is an especially useful form of communications for short messages between two participants, such as "Please finish the report." Electronic mail is an increasingly popular way to link people who have common interests or problems and who are located in different parts of an organization.

Initial discussions via computer networking become a basis for exchanging ideas and forming ad hoc groups. In this way, networks can actually facilitate face-to-face exchanges, not simply substitute for them. Keeping in touch also means being able to easily book appointments, schedule meeting places, and reserve equipment.

Another benefit of electronic mail is eliminating telephone tag. Many companies find the greatest advantage of electronic mail is that messages are held until the recipient has time to request them and respond.

The features and applications of electronic mail make it a viable service for tenants in an intelligent building. Some of the more common commands for sending it are:

- Send message—puts message in receiver's . . . "pigeon hole" on the computer.
- Forward message—allows a message to be read and passed along to one or more readers.
- Quit—allows user to stop and leave the mail system.
- Help—brings in information regarding use of features and instructions.
- Timed message delivery—allows sender to create a message for future delivery. This feature can be used as a time reminder for the user.
- Group—allows message distribution to a group of people.
- Copy—sends carbon or blind copies.
- Registered/forced reply—permits sender to be informed when a message has been received and, in some cases, forces the recipient to reply to the message.

Typical features for reading or receiving mail are:

- Acknowledged or received—tells the sender that the message was received and allows a reply.
- Again—permits the message to be read again.
- Print—tells the computer to print the message on a hard copy printer.
- Hold—indicates the recipient received the message, has no reply at this time, but wants to hold the message until later.

- Save/File/Copy/Delete—puts the message into a permanent filing area or the electronic waste basket.
- Append—permits a note to be attached to the bottom of a previously written message.
- Reply—Sends a message that can be appended with comments, then sent to its final disposition.

These features are slightly different in each electronic mail system. For example, some systems provide the writer with a menu listing. This is easier to use than entering a complicated list of commands. The myriad of other features found on electronic mail systems provide multilevel passwords, listings of messages sent or received, verification of messages, and priority messages.

The development of a universal electronic mail network is facilitated by the growth in numbers of intelligent buildings. Such buildings act as natural nodes in an electronic mail network, since they house automated offices. Commercial systems such as Western Union's EasyLink Service are designed to link otherwise incompatible electronic mail systems, speeding the creation of a universal electronic mail network.

Facsimile

Facsimile, often called fax, is an electronic mail system used primarily for transmitting copies of photographs, documents with signatures, sheets of numerical or financial data, and graphics (see Figure 3-4). Some organizations, such as law firms, accounting firms, and sales offices, find fax essential to their business and to communicating with clients.

A scanning device picks up the facsimile of a document and translates it into signals, which are sent over the telephone to a similar machine at the destination. The original that is fed into the equipment and processed for transmission is returned. This is similar to photocopying.

Facsimile provides an alternative to the postal system for the rapid transfer of hard copy materials at a reasonable cost. Corporations are using fax to transmit documents between offices. This allows them to utilize the expertise of individuals in different geographic locations in the preparation of a project or study without the delays associated with mailing documents between offices and the expense of express delivery services. In addition, most advanced facsimile models allow interface with word pro-

FIGURE 3–4

NEC's BIT 1 Facsimile Machine sends copies of documents in 12 seconds with a single touch.

Photo courtesy of NEC

cessors or other computer systems. This interface capability further facilitates the transmission of lengthy documents and reduces equipment expenses for firms with light facsimile volume.

The desired facsimile features are digital transmission, white-line skipping, and automatic send and receive capabilities. Digital transmission and white-line skipping contribute to rapid transmission speeds. Automatic send and receive capabilities allow multi-page documents to be sent automatically and received at an unattended terminal.

Copiers

The copier is another office machine recently modified to allow communications. Intelligent copiers can now receive data from a computer on a magnetic tape or by direct connection. Multiple copies can then be made automatically, thereby saving operating and printer time. In the future, these devices will be able to communicate with other equipment such as personal computers, combining copier and facsimile functions.

On-Line Database Access

On-line services or information utilities provide databases that offer vast libraries of information to subscribers using communicating devices (see Figure 3–5). More managers are using on-line sources to access vital business information quickly (see Figure 3–6).

Commercial databases contain information such as data on the political and economic environment, business competitors, customers, new products, and new markets. Almost all on-line databases are derived from existing printed sources, such as periodicals, reference works, and other documents familiar to managers and executives, and provide more convenient access to these sources.

Three major examples of on-line information suppliers are:

CompuServe:
- Special Interest Groups (SIGs): More than 50 electronic "clubs" meet on-line and exchange views and information about almost any subject.
- Encyclopedias: *Grolier's Academic American* with a 9-million-word database of more than 29,000 subject entries and the *World Book Encyclopedia*, including 31,000 subject entries and more than 10 million words of text.
- Business Services: Figures on more than 9,000 securities are

---

FIGURE 3–5 Communications Devices for Accessing Databases

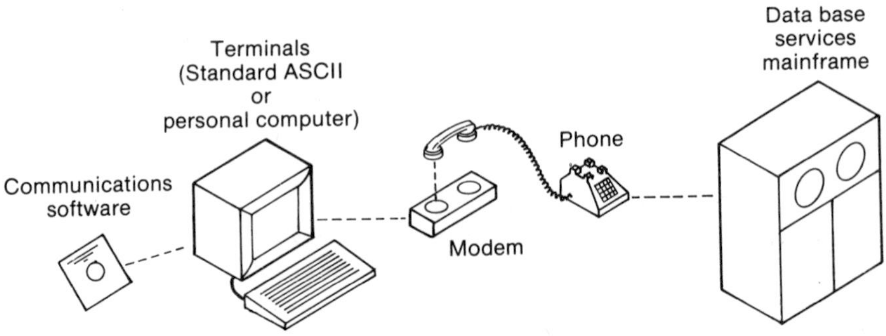

FIGURE 3–6

Managers can use online sources to access vital information quickly.

updated every 20 minutes throughout each trading day. Also provides detailed descriptive and financial information on thousands of major publicly held companies and current and historical information on more than 40,000 stocks, bonds, and options. Gives specialized reports on commodities, today's economy, and implications for the future. Financial commentaries from the nation's leading business and news publications are available as well.

• Information On Demand (IOD): Provides access to professional research services. Will investigate, for a fee, any topic of interest in the news media and professional journals.

Performs market and technical research and provides, at a special rate, translations of foreign technical material into English.

The Source:

- Electronic Mail: Each subscriber has an electronic mailbox addressed by account number and all previously mentioned benefits. It can be used while on the road for communicating with the home office and field representatives, to stay in touch with clients and suppliers, or to send messages to friends and relatives.
- Computer Conferencing: A conference can include from 2 to 200 participants who engage in business meetings or committee discussions. (See Computer Teleconferencing p. 51.)
- Chat: Fellow subscriber Source members can meet and communicate electronically, often for less than the cost of a telephone call.
- News and Sports: Associated Press Videotex service provides 250 daily dispatches on national and international sports, business, and weather news.
- Retrieval and Research: Subscribers can order any book in print electronically. Also available are summaries from 27 leading business publications such as *Forbes*, *Venture*, and *Harvard Business Review*. Customized research can be ordered for a fee.

Dow Jones News Retrieval Service:

Dow Jones is slightly different from any other on-line vendor in America. Subscribers can choose from among 26 databases in four categories:

- Business and economic news.
- Financial and investment services.
- Dow Jones quotes.
- General news and information.

It also provides quotations with a minimum 15-minute delay during market hours. A full year's worth of daily volume is provided; high, low, and closing figures; monthly summaries going back five years; and quarterly summaries for the past four years. Its on-line information features entire texts of *The Wall Street Journal* and *Barron's* for the last several months.

Videotex

Videotex is an interactive technology allowing users to send and receive text and graphics via either a personal computer or a keyboard and decoder unit attached to a television set. To intelligent building tenants, videotex presents an on-line information service used to gain access to databases throughout the world (see Figure 3–7).

The most attractive aspect of videotex is its simplicity. Simple menus and prompts access information from a videotex database. The information, whether text, charts, or pictures, is displayed in a single-frame format, much like the index of a book. No computer knowledge or programming expertise is required of the user, and easy information retrieval means fast access. The system apportions only a small amount of computer time for this service, hence costs for it are low.

In the U.S., videotex was first marketed to individual consumers. Home videotex promised consumers the ability to bank and shop via terminals connected to their television sets. However, only two consumer systems are presently in operation—Knight-Ridder Newspapers' Viewtron System and The Times Mirror Videotex Services' Gateway System. This has prompted many industry watchers to suggest that home videotex is mostly talk and little action. It is, instead, within the corporate world that videotex use is expected to grow.

Case Study—Pacific Bell

Pacific Bell launched an in-house videotex system, dubbed Info-Pac, in January of 1984. The regional Bell operating company's goal in con-

---

FIGURE 3–7 Videotex—Another Online Information Service.

Videotex service

Information provider   Data base   Consumer

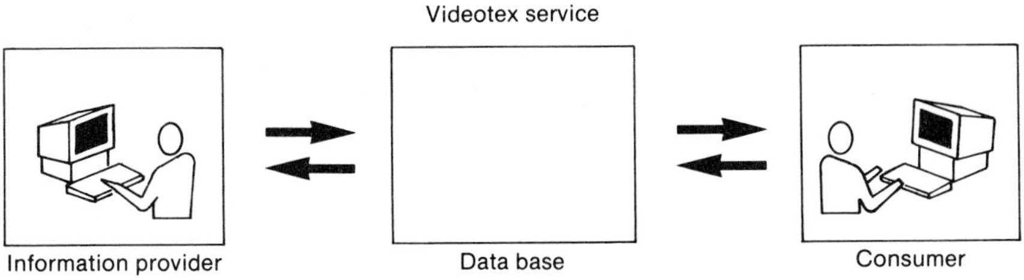

structing the system was to acquire a working knowledge of the technology. This was based on data that showed videotex would become the network traffic of the future and the realization that an understanding of it acquired through hands-on expertise was necessary.

The system is used almost exclusively by Pacific Bell's senior management personnel and currently features company and marketing news, a list of area seminars and conventions of interest to Pacific Bell's major accounts, electronic messages, and a list of news stories of interest to the company's department managers. Many vendors visualize companies using their videotex systems to provide employees with an inexpensive medium for rapidly distributing timely information.

Experts agree that many videotex vendors have focused their efforts on packaging this technology as a new information system designed for corporate sector use. Thus they are currently referred to as private, in-house videotex systems. Digital Equipment Corp. (DEC), AT&T Information Systems, Inc. and Honeywell, Inc. have all unveiled a variety of hardware and software videotex products. These announcements served to promote videotex as a viable corporate information system.

The novel feature of IBM and DEC offerings is that they converge on the concept of the personal computer as the videotex workstation. In contrast, AT&T and Honeywell videotex systems are based on the use of a dedicated terminal. The advantage of the IBM and DEC videotex systems in an intelligent building is that they allow tenants to take advantage of their installed base of user terminals, therefore eliminating the need to purchase additional hardware.

Teleconferencing

Teleconferencing systems enable two or more individuals at two or more locations to communicate. Without having to interrupt their work schedules and without having to pay for costly travel, these individuals can exchange verbal and visual information and examine texts, drawings, plans, or sketches.

Teleconferencing has become increasingly important as a substitute for more traditional forms of corporate communication. It is a viable alternative to face-to-face meetings, allowing for an easy exchange of information without the expensive time-wasting formalities of traditional corporate meetings. One third of these meetings appear to be for the sole purpose of exchanging information, and not for decision making. In fact, once most meetings and conferences are stripped of small tasks and formalities, their useful duration is usually less than one half hour. The most expensive element in operating an office is communications. (This broad category includes everything from answering telephones and posting notices on bulletin boards, to writing letters and participating in meetings and conferences.) Managers concerned with reducing operating costs and increasing productivity are looking for more cost-effective methods of communicating.

According to comprehensive management studies, executives and managers spend 65 percent of their time communicating. That is, they spend more than six hours each workday attending meetings, reporting on those meetings, and talking on the phone. Only about 20 percent of an executive's or manager's time is spent doing desk work. Moreover, 60 percent of all communications do not require face-to-face meetings, and topics discussed in meetings can often be handled in less costly ways.[1]

Due to increasing costs of traditional forms of organizational communications, advances in technology, and the benefits of teleconferencing, executives and managers are turning increasingly to teleconferencing for speedier and more effective communication.

The basic types of electronic teleconferencing are:

- Radio.
- Video.
- Slow-scan television.
- Audio.
- Computer.

Radio teleconferencing. The key considerations when using radio-based or over-the-air teleconferencing are:

- Good for transmission over widely dispersed areas.
- Low cost when compared to stringing wire.
- Cannot be used when security is required.
- Requires special high-frequency receivers.
- Can also be used as a paging system.
- Can be connected to the telephone network.

Video teleconferencing. Full-motion video teleconferencing allows people in two or more locations to have contact, almost as if they were seated in the same room. This form of teleconferencing is attractive to many people, economics aside, because it closely resembles face-to-face meetings. Such a resemblance is particularly effective when the message contains more than just the facts, when it is important to project the emotions behind the facts and the urgency and intensity of a message. Research indicates that fully 65 percent of all information received by the brain is nonverbal.[2]

Some of the key features of video teleconferencing are:

• There is real-time delivery of video images.
• It allows for personal presence.
• It imparts body language and immediate emotions.
• It allows for rapid decision making.
• It is ideal for group discussions, as opposed to one-to-one conversations.
• It allows for crisis meetings to take place quickly.
• It allows for high impact Hollywood-style events.
• It requires large capital commitment.
• It requires large, ongoing overhead and maintenance.

Slow-Scan television. Some slow-scan teleconferencing features are:

• Uses normal telephone lines rather than broadband circuits.
• Provides portability and usability at remote sites.
• Provides non-moving pictures—presentations are similar to a 35mm slide show.
• Provides pictures or presentations that can be recorded on audio cassette recorders or computer disks for later use.
• Availability of low- and high-resolution systems, taking from two to over seven minutes per image.
• Very low cost, compared to full-motion video.

Audio teleconferencing. Audio teleconferencing uses telephones to carry out two-or-more-way voice communications among people who are geographically separate. Audio teleconferences can be assembled in one of two ways: (1) by dialing out from the audio bridge or (2) by dialing into the bridge. In the dial-out process, a conference operator or controller calls all participants sequentially during a short period prior to the meeting and bridges or connects them until all are assembled. However, a dial-out system can take up to 30 minutes to arrange.

In the dial-in process, individual teleconferees call to a "meet me" bridge at a specified time. This reduces a meeting set-up time by eliminating major delays, e.g., incorrect telephone numbers, unavailability to take the call, and poor connections. Audio teleconferencing can be a powerful, inexpensive communications tool. Some of the more viable applications of audio teleconferencing include:

- Coordination of internal administrative affairs.
- Interfacing with field offices.
- Product releases and telemarketing.
- Training of field personnel.
- Coordination of remote manufacturing/operations.
- Corporate relations and product development.

Audio teleconferencing can be expanded to include visual materials through the addition of a facsimile machine in teleconference rooms. Facsimile can be used to send documents to participants when needed. Rooms equipped with personal computers can add the extra visual dimension of computer-generated graphics.

Computer teleconferencing (CT).   Computer teleconferencing offers the following advantages to the corporation:

- CT is the lowest priced of the teleconferencing technologies.
- CT uses more creative software systems in developing models for better decision making. With the growing emphasis on decision support systems, expert systems, artificial intelligence (AI), and management tools for graphic display of information, CT accommodates newer modeling systems without radically changing user interaction.
- CT provides the key advantage of long-term record and electronic filing.
- Interruptions from telephone calls are reduced. Information is passed when the recipient is ready to accept it.
- The ability to organize message and responses, allowing for the most logical presentation, is improved. The discipline of putting thoughts into writing before communicating them improves the quality of communications.
- Electronic "footprints" keep everyone involved in a project informed from beginning to end. People can enter the process at any point and have full documentation to evaluate the process to date.

CHAPTER FOUR

The Building Information Center

INTRODUCTION

Intelligent buildings provide a range of facilities and services to tenants through the Building Information Center (BIC) (see Figure 4-1). Services available through such a center include:

FIGURE 4-1   Range of Shared Services

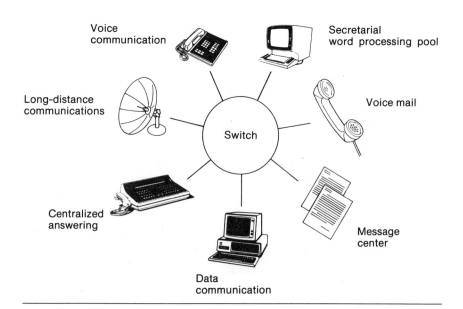

Shared services

Voice communication

Secretarial word processing pool

Long-distance communications

Voice mail

Switch

Centralized answering

Message center

Data communication

- Sale, rent, or lease of information equipment.
- Shared tenant services:
  - Office services.
  - Tenant/text—directory and information service.
  - Message center.
  - Modem pooling.
  - 800 number inbound and WATS line outbound.
  - Network interface—CATV.
  - Encryption—systems security.
  - Archival storage—vault and on-line storage.
- Tenant services training—the demonstration center.

In addition to information systems services, many intelligent buildings offer the concierge services that hotels have specialized in for so long. These can be considered intelligent resources, and include:

- Building concierge.
- Temporary space rental.
- Conference and "war" room facilities.
- Consulting services.
- Temporary and full-time secretarial support.
- Overnight package delivery.
- Office supplies.

The BIC provides tenants with all the above services through one central location. And tenants can tailor their use according to their needs. The following sections describe these services and how they benefit tenants and developers alike.

SALE, RENT, OR LEASE OF EQUIPMENT

Tenants of an intelligent building may not yet have their own office automation (OA) equipment and need to rent or lease devices which are fully compatible with the building's information network. Those wanting to purchase their own equipment can do so through the BIC. Not only will this equipment be fully compatible with other building information systems, BIC support staff can train personnel and maintain new equipment (see section "Tenant Services Training—The Demonstration Center").

Tenants who want to approach office automation on a more experimental level can rent or lease devices from the BIC without being locked into a potentially inappropriate choice while using various office automation equipment.

Whether tenants choose to buy, rent, or lease OA equipment, they gain access to the services which intelligent buildings offer their tenants on a shared basis (discussed in Chapter 3). By sharing services, tenants pay less than if they had obtained the services individually. Developers still realize a profit while providing these services at a lower rate to tenants. This is done through obtaining discounted bulk rate services. The combined needs of tenants of an intelligent building push building services into higher levels, which cost less than individual subscriptions or purchases.

Developers also earn revenue from the sale, rent, or lease of equipment. In addition, they earn revenue by providing support in the form of training and maintenance. Ultimately, the degree to which tenants use shared tenant services determines the profitability of intelligent buildings.

SHARED TENANT SERVICES

In some cases, tenant needs do not justify the rent, lease, or purchase of OA equipment. A BIC can then provide tenants with the equipment and services to meet their limited needs. These can take the form of shared word processing, facsimile, high-speed copiers, and many of the other OA tools. Time and cost savings benefit tenants since equipment is located within the building, and they pay only for facilities they use. Tenants can purchase and use services needed regularly and then use the BIC to meet their less frequent needs.

The building developer also gains. Services such as electronic mail and subscriptions to on-line databases can be provided to tenants on an as-used basis, generating income in addition to that received by providing equipment. Furthermore, as tenants are exposed to information technology through the BIC, developers benefit by the increased use of building information systems. Since the profitability of intelligent buildings depends on providing services to tenants, the BIC can play a large part in determining the financial success of intelligent buildings. The following sections describe the equipment and services available to tenants on a shared basis through a BIC.

Office Services

Word processing. Word processing support can be provided to tenants through the BIC. Such support involves providing the equipment itself and operators. For instance, on-site personnel can process typing requests on an hourly basis, as well as pick up and deliver the finished product. As in the case of facsimile, the benefits of word processing can be enjoyed by tenants who cannot cost-justify the purchase, rental, or leasing of word processing equipment.

Facsimile. Facsimile machines (see Chapter 3), or telecopiers, have evolved from machines that took six minutes to send one murky page, to equipment which transmits a letter-size page in as little as 15 seconds. Modern telecopiers are more effective and efficient, and their speed reduces costs of associated telephone calls. This makes it feasible to transmit documents of numerous pages in a short period at a nominal cost.

New facsimile machines, however, are relatively expensive, costing several thousand dollars. They are usually very underused, since the typical small to medium-sized tenant does not generate a high volume of material for transmission. Offered through the BIC on a per-page basis, telecopiers can provide a valuable service to tenants on occasions when they are needed and are a profit generator for building developers/owners. Like facsimile, copiers can be used in an intelligent building on a shared basis through the BIC.

Teleconferencing. Intelligent buildings play a very important part in teleconferencing. Their internal wiring allows for simplified implementation and shared, full-motion video and audio teleconferencing rooms (see Figure 4–2). For example, video teleconferencing is a valuable business tool which could be prohibitively expensive if acquired by tenants individually. Intelligent buildings, linked through satellite and fiber optic transmission mediums, provide an affordable environment to small and medium-sized tenants on a time-available basis. Video teleconferencing facilities that are shared in an intelligent building require a specially equipped room (see Figures 4–3 and 4–4) and a satellite up-link. Typically, use is for 6 to 10 people per location at $500 to

FIGURE 4–2 Video Teleconferencing Room

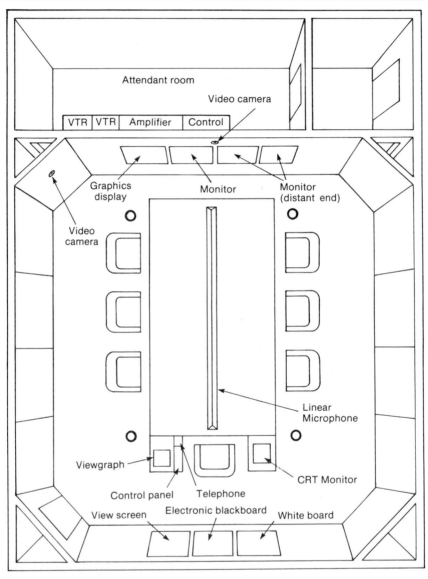

Attendant room

Video camera

| VTR | VTR | Amplifier | Control |

Graphics display

Monitor

Monitor (distant end)

Video camera

Linear Microphone

Viewgraph

CRT Monitor

Control panel Telephone

View screen Electronic blackboard White board

○ Ceiling speakers

FIGURE 4-3

A multipurpose conference room located on the 28th floor of AT&T Headquarters at 550 Madison Avenue, New York City. This facility has sophisticated audio graphics as well as video capabilities. The acoustics of this facility allows for the preparation and transmission of video programs as well as sophisticated tele- and video conferencing.

$8,000 per meeting, depending on duration and transmission distance.

Some approaches to marketing video teleconferencing in the intelligent building or office park are:

- Dedicated—Teleconferencing rooms for exclusive use by a single corporation.
- Semi-dedicated—Teleconferencing rooms primarily used by a single corporation, but available to other members at certain times of the day.
- Shared—Teleconferencing rooms available to tenants by reservation.

Teleconferencing rooms available to tenants through a BIC will speed the growth of this important but underused information medium.

FIGURE 4-4

A portion of the video control center located on the 28th floor of 550 Madison Avenue, New York City. Shown here is the video and audio control and mixing console, as well as video monitors and title generator. This studio is capable of producing video programs.

Audio bridge. For those who are unwilling to pay the costs of full-motion video teleconferencing, intelligent buildings can provide the facilities for audio teleconferences. Audio teleconferencing relies primarily on telephones to carry out two-or-more-way voice communications among people who are geographically separate. The same room which provides video teleconferencing can be equipped with speakerphones and used for this less expensive conferencing system. When numerous sites must be connected, however, an audio bridge is required.

An audio bridge is a device which generally allows up to 48 (or more, depending on which system is used) people to be connected together simultaneously. Telephone lines go into the bridge, where they are amplified, noise is filtered out, and participants given the same sound level in the conference. An operator calls participants or arranges a predetermined time for the teleconference. Once users are linked, the operator pushes the bridge function.

Audio bridges are now automated, allowing participants to hold daily multipoint teleconferences without the need to interface with a conference operator. A microprocessor coupled with a voice synthesizer greets and instructs the participants. As conferees dial into the system, they are greeted by the voice synthesizer and told to introduce themselves to the others. The benefits of an audio bridge system on building premises over "meet me" type audio teleconferences via phone lines include:

- Handling 48 as opposed to 5 users.
- Automatic amplification and noise reduction.
- Does not tie up the phone system.

Access to the system is via touch telephone tones generated by the user's telephone. An audio bridge can include numerous features (see Appendix B).

Audio teleconferencing can be expanded to include visual materials by adding a facsimile machine to the teleconference process. Facsimile can be used to send document copies to participants when needed. Rooms equipped with personal computers can add the extra visual dimension of computer-generated graphics.

Electronic mail. There are many types of electronic mail, some of which are available as multitenant service offerings. In the broadest sense, any system that sends a message or document electronically—from one desk to another or one office to another—can be considered electronic mail. Each of the following concepts is a different type of electronic mail:

- Telex.
- TWX.
- Facsimile.
- Point-to-Point (often called station-to-station) Communications (interoffice).
- Intraoffice Computer Based Mail System (CBMS).
- Message Center—message center with central printer and telephone dispatch.
- Broadband Local Area Network—interfaced with microcomputers, a file server or facsimile machines.
- PBX-Based Electronic Mail.

The first four types of electronic mail involve renting equipment and reselling a local and/or long-distance transmission network to tenants. In addition, some systems require computer processing, storage, protocol conversion, and other functions for which additional fees are charged through the BIC. The last four types of electronic mail are used primarily within an office or building, over the major intelligent building information systems.

On-line database access. On-line services can be of great value to businesses which use them to gain quick and easy access to important information. This (discussed in Chapter 3) requires using a terminal, modem, transmission mediums, and a subscription. While the equipment is integral to the intelligent building, the BIC can acquire subscriptions to major on-line databases and resell them to tenants on an as-used basis. Access is via the intelligent building's host computer, and tenants pay for services as they use them.

Tenant/Text

One application of videotex in an intelligent building is Tenant/ Text, an information dispersal system available from building managers to tenants, among tenants, and from tenants to visitors.

For example, the lobby of the building using Tenant/Text contains a terminal with a menu of all facilities and businesses contained in the building. A visitor easily accesses the system and receives information on services offered by the building and/or tenants, without the time-consuming process of going to each department.

Tenant/Text offers a welcome departure from the traditional static lobby directories. In place of the usual large wall director, the electronic directory requires only a monitor and a small keypad. The Tenant/Text directory allows listing of more information than previously possible because it has an expandable storage capability. Furthermore, updates can be made instantly from the management office. If a tenant moves out, or a name is misspelled, necessary changes take only minutes.

Message Centers

There are several types of message centers. Each has a different application in a multitenant services environment. In its simplest form, message center equipment can be leased to a tenant through the BIC simply as another type of telephone station equipment, with the tenant providing message center operators. This arrangement is generally called a *corporate message center*. Or the message center can be one centralized function that serves many tenants. When a message center serves more than one tenant, it is generally referred to as a *telephone answering service (TAS)*.

Corporate message centers. Large organizations usually want their own staff to operate message centers so they can answer telephone calls for busy or unoccupied extensions. By concentrating the message handling function, they reduce the interruptions of individual secretaries and increase their productivity.

Most message center equipment is capable of storing answer phrases, organizational and personnel directories, and temporary status information so that the message center operators can answer each extension as if they were the secretary for the party being called. They can also activitate message-waiting indicator lamps similar to those in hotels. If the organization uses an internal electronic message or electronic mail system, the message center can keyboard its telephone messages and deliver them electronically. The message center can serve as the first step toward introducing electronic mail systems into organizations and provide another source of revenue for the BIC.

Telephone answering service (TAS). Small companies often want to have a telephone answering service (TAS) as an alternative or backup to a secretary or corporate message center. By having an on-premise message center system connected by a central PBX system, it is feasible to activate message-waiting lamps on telephones in a tenant's office, and cost-effective to have a pool of operators answer any extension for tenants. After a few rings, the call is forwarded to the BIC, where it is answered in the manner a tenant prefers. This service can be billed as it is used.

A message center operated by the BIC is cost-effective when compared to off-premises telephone answering services. These can be very expensive when every extension is treated as a separate customer. The typical competitive telephone answering service charges $35 to $60 per month for each telephone line answered. In addition, when tenants require external call forwarding, an additional telephone company access charge is incurred.

The biggest problem with off-premise answering services, however, is that they do not generally offer a method of activating message-waiting indicators. For this reason, most small companies choose to have only their main telephone extension connected to the answering service and use it only during breaks, lunch hours, and when they are closed. An on-premise TAS removes these limitations.

Voice mail. Voice mail can be made available to tenants through the BIC in conjunction with an operator-based message center. Busy or unanswered calls are first routed to the message-center operators. If the caller wants to leave a message, operators can either record or keyboard it into the video message terminal, depending on how the recipient wants calls delivered. Voice mail increases operators' productivity, extends the operating hours for message delivery, and assures that messages are delivered exactly the way they are left by the caller.

According to Larry Stocket, director of special projects of RealCom, the real estate arm of Satellite Business Systems (SBS),

> Voice mail eliminates pink telephone slips, poor handwriting, and transposed telephone numbers, or alternatively decreases the labor intensity of keyboarding and reading messages back to people when they call in for their messages. The dual capability message center provides the benefits and flexibility of live operators and reduces labor requirements by over 50 percent, freeing operators to handle more calls per operator.[1]

Often, neither voice mail nor a centralized operator message center alone can satisfy everyone in an organization. The combined capability, on the other hand, offers flexibility for tenants who need to have their messages handled by their secretaries and/or backed up by a central message center or a sophisticated answering machine. The combination offers the BIC an opportunity to provide a substantially improved and cost-effective message handling capability.

An important consideration in offering voice mail or message center equipment is providing message-waiting indicators so the party called knows there is a message waiting (see Figure 4.4). While this may seem like a small detail, it is critical to the success of voice mail. It is therefore recommended that voice mail be introduced at the same time as basic telephone service so that telephone instruments with such indicators are installed. When telephone instruments eventually must be changed, or separate message indicators rented, each requires its own power outlet at extra cost.

Modem Pooling

Modem pooling is a potentially valuable BIC tenant service. BIC services where high transmission speeds are required—such as accessing on-line databases—require modems. At higher data rates, modem pooling becomes very cost-effective.

Instead of every tenant having a modem for each telephone, a series of modems operating at different speeds can be shared among tenants (see Figure 4–5). Data interface units (DIUs) necessary for modem pooling would be included (see Figures 4–6 and 4–7). However, if the majority of tenants are satisfied with low data-transmission rates, modem pooling will actually cost them more than when all provide their own modem for each telephone. It is when tenants need higher data rates that modem pooling becomes very cost effective.

Developers must determine whether there is a need for the service before installing a modem pool. If none is currently required, a modem pool can easily be added in the future. Only a

---

FIGURE 4–5 Data Communications/Data Processing Architecture

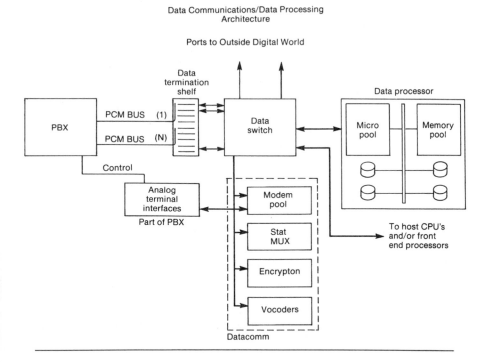

FIGURE 4–6

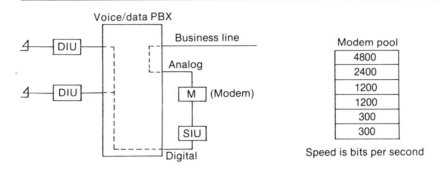

Voice/data PBX

Modem pool

4800
2400
1200
1200
300
300

Speed is bits per second

Individual terminals can be restricted to certain modems in the modem pool through "user class of service." When not restricted, users can choose the data transmission speed best suited for the immediate application.

shelf is required to hold the five or six modems which must be hooked into the PBX (see Figure 4–8).

800 Numbers (Inbound WATS) and WATS Lines (Outbound WATS)

An 800 number in present-day terminology is an inbound WATS (Wide Area Telecommunications Service) line, with the recipient liable for call charges. In the intelligent building, two approaches to WATS services are possible. Tenants can have their own 800

FIGURE 4–7

When each terminal has 6 modems, as opposed to sharing a modem pool, the user is restricted to services which use modems with similar data transmission speeds. For instance, a tenant in an intelligent building with a 1200 6ps modem attached to his or her terminal can access a remote database, or CPU, with a modem speed of 1200 bpu also.

FIGURE 4-8

A portion of the Communications Center on the 28th Floor of 550 Madison Avenue. The background cabinets contain the Data Modem Pool, which will be utilized to eliminate the majority of stand-alone data modem installations. It is estimated that approximately $1 million in yearly cost will be saved via the utilization of the modem pool.

numbers, or buildings can have an 800 number from which calls are transferred to the correct tenant. Each tenant receives an extension number. The same approach is possible in using the outbound WATS, the only difference being the direction of calling.

When tenants share inbound and outbound WATS lines, significant savings can result. WATS line use is prorated, the first block of hours costing more than the next block of hours, and so forth. WATS lines used by many tenants reduces the individual cost of service. Since tenants can be billed on a usage basis, developers can gain revenues from providing 800 numbers and WATS lines.

Network Interface—CATV

Traditionally, cable television systems have offered only home television service. Cable TV can mean more than one-way entertainment, however. As a recent report from Strategic of San Jose, California, noted,

> CATV is driving hard to become the first supplier of universal broadband, integrated communications networks capable of simultaneously transmitting two-way voice, data and video signals. . . . [CATV can play] a major role in the development of such a universal communications service before the turn of the century. The market for these services is expected to be greater than the market for telephone services today. In fact, the new system might well absorb telephone services as we know them.[2]

A major attraction of cable systems is their advantage over other data communications systems in moving data at high rates. Using normal telephone carriers is currently very expensive. CATV would reduce these costs. CATV is a viable approach to moving data within a city.

The major cost associated with CATV is the initial hook-up fee, which can be shared among tenants when CATV is provided through the BIC.

Encryption—Systems Security

Encryption, or coding, is a mathematical algorithm. An encryption algorithm is a method of computation based on a prime number sequence that actually scrambles the data as it comes in. A key code changes the method the algorithm uses to scramble the clear text that comes in. As the key changes, the same data is scrambled differently. Some products have a 128-character key. In 128 characters, there are approximately a trillion combinations of prime numbers, supplying an ample number of codes.

Security issues arise from the financial nature of business information. Annual reports that reflect a company's financial status, information transmitted between company locations, government contract bids, and sales reports transmitted from field locations to company headquarters can all be vital and confidential.

The first part of the security problem is right at the desk and has nothing to do with criminality. It may only be company confidential, such as personnel and payroll data, medical reports, or information tenants are tracking on their competition, or real secrets like proprietary programs.

Senior executives responsible for protecting valuable information regarding products, processes, and corporate negotiations have long worried about the vulnerability of proprietary data. In the highly competitive environment of the 1980s, this concern rapidly translates into crash programs to find ways to maintain the everyday flow of business, yet hide data—which can include letters and memos as well as statistical materials—from unauthorized readers. With micros now connected to mainframes, the accessibility of data to snoopers both inside and outside corporations is enormous.

Criminal or competitive espionage is another reason to be concerned with systems security. Some security specialists believe it is a problem where there is more going on than is publicly known. In computer information theft, it takes a technician to catch a technician. The people conducting criminal or competitive espionage are extremely intelligent, and companies find out too late when there has been pilfering. It is, therefore, very difficult to catch these people.

Many computer systems today are password protected. This is the locked-door concept: access to the system is denied, while data is left in its original form. Such systems are structured to control access to the mainframe computer rather than securing the data itself. Some argue that encryption is the only means of controlling data flow and securing it. For instance, John E. Martin, director of software development for the Phoenix operations of Honeywell, said, ". . . systems that are based on limiting access to data are the systems that are currently being broken into by the '414 Gang.'"[3] The 414 Gang was a group of Milwaukee teens that gained access to several "secure" databases during the summer of 1983. Such computer criminals are commonly referred to as *hackers*, although hackers are those people who spend a great deal of time at a terminal and are not necessarily thieves.

Encryption costs. An intelligent modem can serve as an encryption device. It has the characteristics of such devices, i.e., the capability to transmit data from one personal computer to another or from a personal computer to a mainframe. An intelligent modem can "front end" both the mainframe and the personal computer, encrypting the data in a way that is totally transparent to both. Neither the host nor the PC is aware that encryption is taking place. Modems which perform this function fall in the $800 to $900 price range. In an intelligent building with a modem pool, tenants can share these devices.

An encryption device, as opposed to a modem, is another choice. However, such products on the market today run from $12,000 to $50,000 a unit. Such a product will encrypt data during transmission and will protect the host itself (the data or voice/data PBX). Either way, the cost of encryption is shared among tenants, and security concerns are met through the BIC.

Archival Storage

Archival storage includes both the traditional vault that stores paper or microfilm and on-line storage of information in computer files.

Vault storage. Given the number and variety of high-tech on-line storage systems, are we really heading toward a realization of the paperless office? Many believe paper will continue to be a key element in business because people are more comfortable with storing and retrieving it. In fact, office automation is actually responsible for the growth in paper files. It is important to remember that prices quoted provide only a rough idea of costs, which are falling daily. The cost of compact copiers and personal computers is decreasing, encouraging more purchases of these paper-generating devices. Paper has been—and, in many cases, remains—the primary information-storage medium for most businesses. According to senior consultant Joseph Pierce, nearly one billion pages of business-related information (including computer-generated hard copy) are processed each day in the United States by 50 million white-collar employees.[4]

How do businesses avoid being buried beneath an avalance of paper? The first step is to establish a well-managed system of hard-copy storage. If the original documents cannot be controlled, control of any subsequent form is questionable. Intelligent buildings can offer original-document storage to tenants. Well managed in conjunction with on-line storage systems, a central archival vault minimizes the amount of expensive space necessary for storage of hard copy.

On-line storage. The OA environment is changing some of the concepts and attitudes about record keeping. Paper-based filing systems have recently been making way for other, high-tech forms of record management. These include computer-output microfilm (COM), computer-assisted retrieval (CAR), and electronic and optical-disk storage. The transition from paper-intensive filing systems to a mix of hard copy, micrographics, and electronic storage is being facilitated by products that store a variety of media.

Micrographics has undergone tremendous change. Before the advent of intelligent microfilmers, computer-assisted retrieval systems, and microfilm jackets, micrographics was considered an archival technology. Present microfilm systems allow updating of stored information, earning them recognition as an active storage medium.[5]

The key to these systems is computer control. Computer indexing of microfilm files and computer-assisted retrieval is made possible by software which allows random input of information and permits its quick retrieval. A computer-assisted retrieval system is one way to manage large volumes of files which tenants can choose to store in the intelligent building's archives.

A confluence of micrographics and data processing uses microprocessor intelligence to index and retrieve documents that are stored on microfilm. Thus, the speed of computer-assisted retrieval (about five seconds) is combined with the low-cost and voluminous storage capabilities of microfilm.

Optical-disk technology is another storage medium still being developed. Optical disks record and read information through the use of a laser-generated binary code. Such systems "promise to play a pivotal role in the business information-management function of the future," according to Dr. David Wolf, national systems support manager in A. B. Dick's Records Systems Division.[6] In its present state, optical-disk technology has these attractions:

- Low-cost storage per megabyte.
- Durability: Data recorded on an optical disk is thought to be safe for at least 10 years.
- Easy to automate in the form of an optical-disk "jukebox."

An intelligent building will contain some form of these vault and on-line storage mediums. Renting excess capacity to tenants through a BIC provides revenues for building managers and a valuable service to space-conscious tenants. In addition, the special needs of these mixed-storage systems can be met efficiently.

TENANT SUPPORT AND TRAINING:
THE DEMONSTRATION CENTER (DC)

One way to gradually change tenant attitudes about automation and computerization is to set up a demonstration center (DC) in an intelligent building. Such a center can introduce technology three to five years before it appears in the office. This time lag gives a tenant a chance to grow accustomed to the new technology and evaluate it. Employees can learn to operate equipment long before they must use it on their jobs (see Figure 4–9). Tenants have a chance to experiment with all aspects of automation, from user training to communications, so that when the time to automate comes, they are prepared for fully compatible, functional systems.

The demonstration center concept, originally proposed by IBM as a way of making information directly available to end users, is a reality in many companies around the world. More commonly known as *information centers*, but termed *demonstration*

FIGURE 4–9 On-Site Shared Services Center, Arlington, Virginia

Called the Building Information Center (BIC) in this book, it provides tenants with an innovative and economical way to manage their telecommunications information processing and office automation needs.

center here to differentiate it from the Building Information Center, it is one of the most important services that building managers can offer tenants. "It's our feeling that every organization will eventually have an Information Center," says Philip Berg, vice president of Applied Data Research (ADR).[7] Instead of each building tenant having its own demonstration center, this function can be provided through a building Demonstration Center and shared among tenants.

A Demonstration Center provides information systems training and assistance to tenants, making it possible for them to solve their business problems using computers as a resource. Demonstration Center consultants work with end users to help them access computer files, develop their own reports and graphics, use on-line databases, and so forth. The need for such a center is reflected in the following questions tenants typically ask:

- How can I use information tools effectively?
- How can my staff be effectively trained in their use?
- What hardware and software is available to me?
- How can I assess new products before buying, renting, or leasing them?
- How does all my equipment interface with the building information system?
- Who can help me with problems—NOW?

Functions of a Demonstration Center

Demonstration centers provide support services in the planning and integration of a wider range of office automation technologies.

In broad terms, there are two main functions of a demonstration center. One is to provide assistance to tenants who have computing problems. The other is to provide general technical assistance. Each function has certain requirements it should fulfill, such as:

Computing.

- Training and education.
    On-the-job, follow-up training in addition to formal classroom instruction.
- Assistance in developing applications.
- Development of prototype programs.
- Software problem solving.

• Consulting with tenants to determine if particular applications are appropriate for their development.
Technical assistance.

• Guidance in selecting hardware and system software.
• Help in selecting and evaluating applications packages.
• Assistance in choosing query and report languages and/or packages.
• Hardware set-up and use.
• Database (or file) back-up, recovery, and archive guidelines.
• Hardware and software problem diagnosis.
• Hardware repairs.
• Hotline assistance.
• Installation of hardware and software.
• Interface with mainframe: Have the necessary communications software and equipment.
• Provide equipment for hands-on use:
  Learning.
  Production work.
  Specialized software and peripherals.
  Take-out (loaners).
• Provide reference library.
• Equipment repair and maintenance.

The services provided determine DC staffing. Services include teaching, consulting, technical support, planning, evaluation, and administration.

Teaching is a major occupation of the information center staff. Computer Aided Instruction (CAI) eases the burden of finding qualified teachers and makes it possible for a tenant to study alone at a terminal, as opposed to taking classes offered by the DC. CAI allows tenants to learn at their own pace, freeing staff for teaching more advanced material.

Consultants may serve specific user needs, such as giving software information. Additionally, some DCs have a "generalist" consultant, a jack-of-all-trades, who recognizes applications and needs and proposes solutions. The DC staff can include a generalist who, after proposing a solution, turns the tenant over to a product or general consultant. The DC's scope should include in-depth knowledge and use of products, evaluation of new products for potential installation, administration, and system measurement.

The Demonstration Center Support Staff

Appropriately staffing a DC is vital. Personnel should have a background in communications, business problem-solving techniques, and productivity tools. The DC staff must also be able to relate quickly to tenants at their level. The DC staff must be made up of communicators who feel comfortable communicating across organizational lines, outside of formal channels, and at all levels— from executive management down (see Figure 4–10).

INTELLIGENT RESOURCES

Building concierge. Hotels have long specialized in such concierge-type services as procuring theater tickets. Intelligent buildings can also offer this type of "soft" information service to tenants. As part of the Building Information Center, building

---

FIGURE 4–10 Demonstration Center Staff

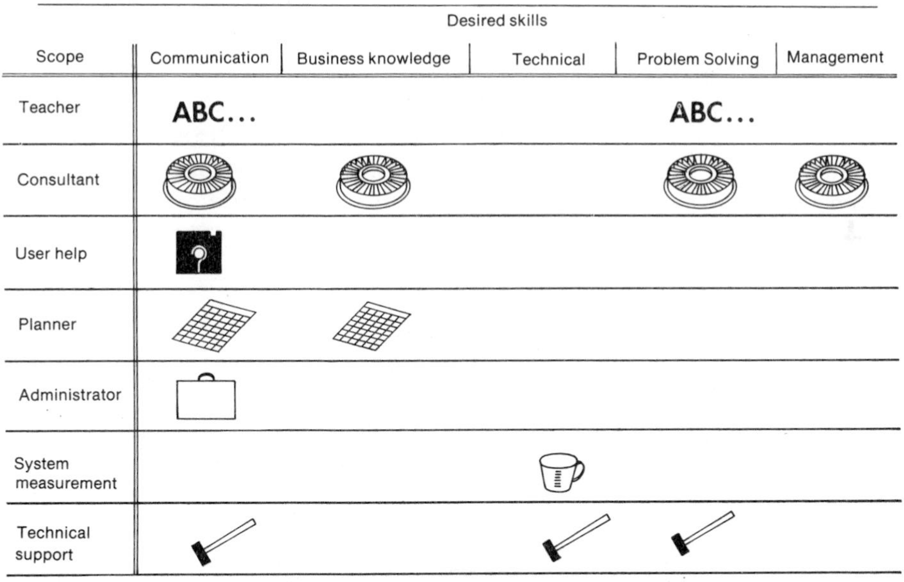

Scope	Desired skills				
	Communication	Business knowledge	Technical	Problem Solving	Management
Teacher	ABC...			ABC...	
Consultant	🌀	🌀		🌀	🌀
User help	▣				
Planner	▤	▤			
Administrator	💼				
System measurement			🥤		
Technical support	🔨			🔨	🔨

The skills needed in an information center sort themselves into five areas, with communication being the most needed. The jobs sort themselves into seven categories (under "scope") with consultant being the one that requires the largest number of skills.

concierge staff have access to and can create their own computer databases of events, theaters, restaurants, limousine services, and so forth. Using such services, tenants are saved the time-consuming process of conducting their own research, while such a service benefits developers both by attracting tenants and by providing a source of revenues. Tenants can be charged on a time-cost basis (i.e., the time it takes to fulfill their needs is charged at a constant rate, plus computer support expenses).

Temporary space rental. Intelligent buildings can offer space to businesses on a temporary basis.

Conference and "war" room facilities. Conference rooms sit vacant most of the time, wasting valuable space and rent. Tenants can lease conference rooms by the hour for important meetings or luncheons from the Building Information Center.

Temporary and full-time secretarial support services. These can be provided through BIC on an hourly, daily, or weekly basis as backup personnel to handle rush proposals, unscheduled workload, or staffwork during vacations or illness.

Interior design services (CAD/CAM). Through staff interior design consultants, a BIC can completely design tenants' offices: from wall covering to ergonomic workstations, from pictures to the latest lighting concepts. These make the office attractive, comfortable, and productive to employees, clients, and guests.

Office supplies. The BIC can function as a general office supply store, selling traditional information tools such as pens and paper. Having an office supply store in the building saves tenants time, especially since the store can deliver orders to tenants.

CHAPTER FIVE

The multitenant communications system forms the hub of the intelligent building.
William S. Herald

Intelligent Building Information Systems

An intelligent building information system is comprised of four major components:

- Telecommunications—PBX or CENTREX.
- Data networking.
- Local area networks (LANs) and other transmission mediums.
- Short- and long-haul networks.

This chapter discusses the features of these systems independently of each other. Chapter 7 discusses the integration of these systems with the building automation systems covered in Chapter 6.

TELECOMMUNICATIONS

Telecommunications is central to a multitenant intelligent building. The principal components of basic telephone service are:

- Telephone equipment.
- Local telephone service.
- Long-distance telephone service.
- Maintenance and administration.

More sophisticated telecommunications services may include features which allow for call accounting and least-cost routing, as well as support of office-automation equipment. In many cases,

75

an integrated voice/data switch provides tenants of an intelligent building with access to a range of services available over the familiar telephone network. The primary telecommunications component in an intelligent building is an advanced digital switch.

The term *switch* is a holdover from the manually operated switchboards of early telephony. *Switching* refers to the process of interconnecting callers at a central point. When callers want to talk to each other, their respective wire pairs or links are interconnected at the central switch. Each telephone needs only to be linked to a central office for full interconnection of all telephones. Thus, if 100 telephones make up a network, only one hundred links are necessary. A switch makes use of star network topology (see Figure 5-1), so named because its design represents the spokes of a wheel radiating from the switch to connected devices.

The alternative to a switching device is a mesh network in which all telephones or stations are connected directly to all other telephones or stations. Thus, in a mesh network, the number of links goes up as rapidly as telephones are added (see Figure 5-2). Because these links are an expensive part of any network, the savings in transmission costs of the star network over the mesh network is obvious. This switching versus transmission tradeoff is fundamental to communications system design and optimization.

FIGURE 5-1 Switches Make Use of Star Network Topology

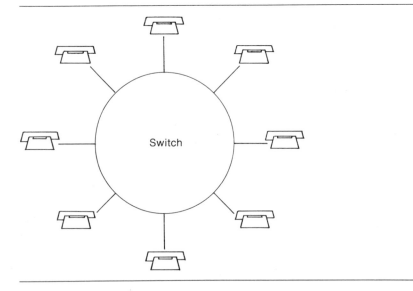

FIGURE 5–2 Switching versus Transmission Tradeoff

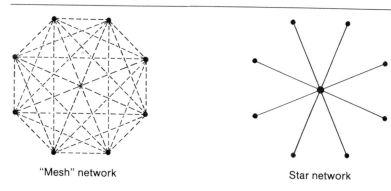

"Mesh" network   Star network

The mesh network uses a great deal of expensive transmission medium, while the star network makes use of a central switching point.

Two basic switching systems can be used to network an intelligent building in a comprehensive, cost-effective manner. These are the Private Branch Exchange (PBX) and CENTREX systems. One of these network switching methods must provide basic telephone service to tenants. PBXs and CENTREX differ in equipment, location, and, to a degree, in the services they provide. The choice between them depends on individual building needs and owner/manager preferences.

There are advantages and disadvantages to both PBXs and CENTREX. There is no one right answer, only lower- and higher-risk choices. Users can choose between a wide variety of switches, depending on individual needs and budgets.

The Private Branch Exchange (PBX)

A PBX is a small switch connected to, or branched off from, a larger switch, (see Figure 5–3). The larger switch is most commonly located on local telephone company premises. The PBX is, therefore, the in-house equivalent of a telephone company central office switch (CO). In its operations, the intelligent building functions in quite the same manner as a telephone company's central office (see Figure 5–4).

PBX financial benefits. A PBX provides an intelligent building with the benefits that star networks use in the public

FIGURE 5-3

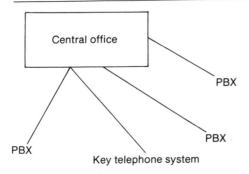

A PBX is a small switch connected to, or branched off a larger switch.

telephone network supplied to individuals. Individual wire pairs from all equipment in the network are connected to the PBX for switching, as opposed to being transmitted individually to the telephone company central office (CO). The benefits of sharing telephone lines mean that fewer lines to the central office are needed and access charges are reduced. As an example, only 10 lines, or trunks, may be required for every 100 telephones. As a result of the AT&T divestiture, access charges for business telephone lines are approximately $2.00 per month per line. Tenants in intelligent buildings benefit by paying lower trunk access charges, while utilizing the newest technology of high speed data transmission and software features.

An Example of PBX Financial Benefits:

The World Trade Center, with its 44,324 access lines, is an example of the financial benefits that result from using a PBX. If it were to become an intelligent building, an aggregation of its main stations would sharply reduce access line costs. In comparison, Cheyenne, Wyoming, the largest city in a state served by Mountain Bell, has only 33,260 access lines.

PBX technical benefits. Tenants whose business productivity and profits depend on communications also benefit technically from using an integrated voice/data switch (see Appendix C for

FIGURE 5-4

A portion of the PBX room located on the 6th Floor at 550 Madison Avenue. Shown in the background is the AT&T Information Systems standard wiring plan, which is utilized to bring telephone service to every desk in the building.

integrated voice/data features). Office automation devices and their links depend on a central PBX switch with enough processing power to serve these varied equipment needs. These needs include more than traditional voice traffic, however. Terminals may be linked to computers, to each other, and to outside networks. These and other devices are more efficiently and economically used when shared, rather than dedicated to individual users. Sophisticated building energy and security systems can also be linked via PBX equipment to sensors throughout a facility.

These features are made possible by recent advances in digital technology, of which the most important emerging capability is high-speed voice/data switching (see Appendix D for discussion on PBX generations).

Presently, most corporations have several expensive voice and data networks. When the telephone and computer systems now in place were acquired, there was very little concern with voice and data integration since it was not generally available. Two underlying factors promoting development of voice/data integration were:

- The need for personal computers, word processors, and other office automation systems connected to on-site mainframe or distant time-sharing computers to provide better and more sophisticated service.
- The ability to contain or control wiring costs.

PBX networking benefits. The features and capabilities inherent to network switching provide numerous benefits to organizations and their employees. Among these benefits are:

- Reduced communications costs:
  Long-distance alternatives.
  Lower numbers of access line charges.
- Simplified billing:
  One bill for all services used.
- Centralized management control of facilities:
  Energy management.
  Security.
- Increased user convenience.
- Reliability of communications facilities.
- Improved transmission.
- Equipment compatibility.
- Simplified maintenance and administration of communications facilities.

Once a digital PBX is installed, it is relatively easy to add data capability to the system. Data connections can be added as they are needed, which simplifies planning and managing data traffic. As more data lines are installed, more processing and memory capacity must be added to the switch. Since this capacity may involve a substantial cost, it must be carefully planned. If the average daily use of the network is low, then the cost contributed by the switch is also low, and network costs are moderate.

The PBX solution may therefore be particularly useful in an office environment where terminal use is low. It is estimated that average office workers use their terminals less than 30 minutes per day. Because the majority of expected tenant functions of the intelligent building can be handled by the PBX, it is well suited as the hub of both the intelligent office and the intelligent building.

PBX software features.   Because the PBX interconnects data and word processing equipment, as well as the telephone system, it acts as a hub of the intelligent building and the intelligent offices it houses (see Figure 5–5). In order to provide this interconnection, sophisticated PBX software is needed. As a whole, PBXs offer over 150 features. Individual PBX vendors may offer features to the user in a system configuration designed specifically to meet an organization's requirements. More importantly, these systems can easily be reconfigured to adapt to that organization's changing conditions. This makes the PBX very attractive to developers of multitenant intelligent buildings. (See Appendix E for a listing of PBX networking software features.)

Designs which support both voice and data communications for multilocation applications provide the features, capabilities,

---

FIGURE 5–5   The PBX as the "Hub" of the Intelligent Building

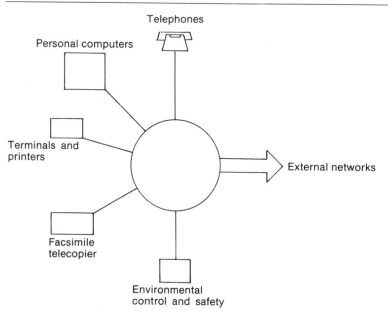

and management control necessary to maintain and operate a voice/data network. Careful consideration should be given during procurement of switching nodes to include compatible network software packages. Many have the following features:

- Automatic route selection.
- Uniform numbering.
- Ring again.
- Traveling class marks.
- Call detail recording.
- Network accessibility software.
- Four-wire switching.
- On and off network calling.
- Digit deletion and insertion.
- Network control center.
- Automatic data speed identification.
- Format and protocol conversion.
- Digital interface unit.
- Account code capability.
- Station message detail recording (SMDR).
- Authorization codes.
- Digital interconnect of remote peripheral equipment.
- Network class of service.
- Network alternate route selection.
- Network signaling.
- Network traffic measurements.
- Queuing:
    Off-hook queuing.
    Call-back queuing.
    Coordinated call-back queuing.
    Call-back queuing to conventional mains.
- Coordinated dialing plan.
- Network authorization codes.
- Network call transfer.
- Traveling class of service.

These features are defined in the glossary at the end of this book. The most important features, however, merit discussion here.

Automatic route selection (ARS). ARS is a feature of advanced PBX systems which determines the most efficient route for completing calls placed across the network. It incorporates many factors for completion of a network call:

- Access codes.
- Uniform dialing plan.
- Automatic least-cost routing.
- Time-of-day routing.
- Automatic on-net to off-net overflow.
- Digit manipulation.
- Network controls.
- Network routing controls.
- Forced bypass.
- Free calling area screening.
- Automatic other common carriers (OCC) access.
- Dial tone detection.
- Network call detail recording.
- Network speed call.
- Supplemental digit restriction.

It is a totally transparent process for the network user. In other words, the user is unaware of the process taking place and need not control it. ARS, the switching system—depending on its degree of sophistication—provides the selection of the most economical circuit to use for outgoing calls. In most systems, this involves the analysis of the first three or six digits dialed by the station user. It bases route selection on look-up tables contained in the switching system memory. These are selected and updated by the building telecommunications manager. The savings from routing a long-distance call via the least expensive route can be large, making automatic route selection an important building developer/manager service offering to tenants.

Station message detail recording (SMDR). SMDR provides tenants with a complete record of telephone use, enabling them to optimize available services. Reports include which extensions placed calls, how long they lasted, destination of calls, and time and date calls were placed. (See Appendix F for listing of SMDR features.)

Toll restriction. Toll restriction is another important software feature. It limits long-distance facilities to only designated telephones, enabling tenants to control long-distance traffic and realize cost savings.

PBXs in the multitenant environment. PBXs are now being developed specifically for the multitenant intelligent building. They offer traditional software functions, switch voice and data digitally, and permit the following:

- Virtually unlimited tenant partitioning. Partitioning provides separate calling privileges and processing for each tenant. It determines the suitability of any switch for multitenant resale purposes. In some systems, up to 512 tenant partitions can be defined in some switches. Each tenant has access to the many resources of the switch.
- Easy access to value-added services. Tenants may share long-distance services and such additional amenities as integrated voice and text message centers or other value-added services. These services can be shared by groups of tenants or configured solely for a single tenant. Access is user friendly, so people benefit from quick and efficient services.
- Optional tenant-to-tenant access. This new software package permits internal calling among tenants within the system.
- Station message detail recording and reporting (SMDR). SMDR information includes specific tenant numbers, partition numbers, and local or long-distance calls made. The system helps tenants identify and control long-distance costs.

A good multitenant communications system makes it easier to attract tenants and to aid profitability through the resale of services.

The CENTREX Offering

CENTREX is a service offered by all Bell operating companies and a handful of independent telephone companies. Two types of CENTREX service exist: CENTREX-CO and CENTREX-CU. The major difference between them lies in the location of the switch.

CENTREX-CO has been the standard service offered. It links each of an organization's telephones to a telephone company central office switch. In contrast, CENTREX-CU combines basic central office service with additional on-premise switching. The same switches found on telephone operating company premises can be installed in the intelligent building.

New CENTREX features. CENTREX now includes over 30 features:
Standard Features:

- Add-on conference—incoming.
- Call transfer—incoming.

- Consecutive station hunting.
- Consultation hold—incoming.
- Direct inward dialing.
- Direct outward dialing.
- Identified outward tolls.
- Interception of calls to unassigned number.
- Station-to-station calling or intercom.
- Touch-tone dialing.

Optional Features:

- Alternate answering.
- Automatic call-back.
- Call forwarding.
- Call hold.
- Call pickup.
- Additional call pickup group.
- Call waiting.
- Dialed conference.
- Distinctive ringing and call waiting tones.
- Loudspeaker paging.
- Off-premise locations.
- Recorded telephone dictation.
- Reminder ring.
- Speed calling.
- Speed dialing.
- Three-way calling (see Appendix G for descriptions).

The major difference between a PBX and central office switch is dependability. Bell telephone switches are the battleships of telephone switching technology. Engineered specifically for reliability, their down time is practically nil. This makes them very attractive to businesses whose losses per minute can run into the thousands of dollars when communications networks fail.

The availability of CENTREX-CU is limited for now, however, because of regulatory issues in each state. Where it is used, CENTREX-CU can be of great benefit to those building developers who do not want to plunge into the telephone business, but do want to have a switch on the premises. Those who wish to fully avoid the concerns of maintenance and down time may opt for CENTREX-CO, since it is wholly maintained on the telephone company premises. As to the appropriateness of central office switches in such applications, telephone operating companies are beginning to realize the needs of intelligent buildings and to develop central-office based switches to handle multitenant building services.

CENTREX provides alternatives to PBXs for developers interested in implementing intelligent buildings and is currently being developed along multitenant lines. The availability of both types of service make it a viable alternative to PBXs. CENTREX, whether located on or off premises, utilizes technology that places a premium on dependability. To many tenants, this is a must in a telecommunications system. Building developers, well aware of tenant needs, may therefore choose CENTREX.

CENTREX was first developed in the early 60s to give large organizations direct dialing capability in and outside of their systems. It eventually evolved to include basic station features such as intercom, call holding, and call transfer. After years of being treated like an unwanted stepchild by AT&T, CENTREX is being marketed with renewed vigor by the divested Bell operating companies (BOCs). The recent flurry of activity surrounding CENTREX has produced:

- A host of new features.
- Attempts by the BOCs before various state commissions to keep CENTREX rates stable and competitive (see Appendix H).
- Efforts at broadening the service's appeal by targeting new markets that the phone companies had previously ignored.

Individually, the Bell operating companies (BOCs) are offering features such as message center, better station message detail recording (SMDR), energy management, automatic route selection, abbreviated dialing, automatic call distribution (ACD, for reservation systems), and electronic key. One CENTREX service permits the customer to have business lines in several locations that are tied into one business network.

An offering called CENTREX Customer Change Feature allows customers to add or delete several features without entering a service order at the telco business office. Such features include call pickup, hold, forwarding, call waiting, abbreviated dialing, and station-controlled conference. Customers can also make changes to allow for:

- Call-forwarding numbers.
- Call pickup groups.
- Class of service.

- Station restrictions.
- Facility restriction-level assignments.

Premium CENTREX. An enhanced version of today's CEN-TREX is being offered by many telephone companies as "Premium CENTREX." Depending on its price and perceived value, this offering could comprise an attractive alternative for companies that are considering scrapping their CENTREX systems.

Telephone companies interested in providing a premium feature package are likely to do so through an "arm's length" subsidiary in order to comply with the provisions of the Modified Final Judgment and the Computer Inquiry II. BOCs are presently allowed to provide only "basic" service in the regulated environment.

The following features are currently found in Premium CEN-TREX:

- Enhanced station message detail recording (SMDR).
- Customer moves and changes.
- 9.6 Kbps switched data transmission.
- Traffic management and reports.
- Electronic telephone instruments.

In addition, a number of enhanced central office features complementing CENTREX will include:

- Voice mail.
- Text electronic mail.
- Energy management.
- Alarms and telemetry.
- Data processing.
- Local area networks.

These are many of the systems inherent to an intelligent building. They make CENTREX a viable alternative to PBXs in cases where building owners want to avoid buying a PBX or want the dependability of a CO switch. (See Appendix I for other possibilities for CENTREX service offerings.)

CENTREX technical benefits. Most CENTREX services can be made available to intelligent buildings and their tenants on central office electronic switch systems (No. 5ESS). Feature-wise, CENTREX is becoming more and more competitive with PBXs. Furthermore, Premium CENTREX is being developed to handle automation of building systems such as energy management, security, fire, and safety.

CENTREX management benefits. CENTREX is attractive to building developers because of its unlimited capacity for growth and ability to handle dynamic swings in volume. As tenants in a building change, the demands placed on telecommunications and other information systems change. Capacity to meet dynamic swings in volume allows for changes in service to meet overall building needs at any given time.

Intelligent buildings are a potentially large market for CENTREX services, whether they are Bell operating company central-office based or corporate-premises based. Besides CENTREX's advantage over PBXs in dependability, there are two other competitive advantages. No capital investment financing is required, and there is no need for building managers to provide maintenance services.

DATA NETWORKING

It is not always cost-effective to connect all terminal users to an integrated voice/data PBX, which typically dedicates only 10 percent of its capacity to data switching. In cases where the extra-building data traffic exceeds this, a data PBX can handle data switching needs in a more cost-effective manner.

In the past, data PBXs were called port selectors, private automatic computer exchanges, data switches, intelligent switches, smart switches, and super contendors, among other names. When integrated voice/data PBXs came on the scene, datacom vendors adopted the name *data PBX* almost universally. The name is concise and appropriate because data PBXs tie computers and terminals together in the same manner that PBXs tie together telephones (and offer many of the same features).

A data PBX allows terminal users to select different computers, or destinations, from their keyboards without moving cables. By queuing those users requesting access to limited ports, expensive computer ports may be shared. Since most people don't use their terminals all day every day, the number of terminals hooked up to a data PBX can be much larger than the number of ports. Users seldom need to wait for a line as they do with an integrated voice/data PBX.

Data PBXs have been around since 1973, having started with the popularity of minicomputers. These minicomputers needed access to other minicomputers or mainframe computers, which data PBXs were designed to provide. The evolution to microcomputers, more commonly known as personal computers (PCs), has fueled the data PBX growth. Personal computers allowed the user to go one step beyond data processing to data communications.

Data Communications

The advent of reliable and relatively inexpensive minicomputers brought on changes in data communications. As minicomputers were distributed throughout organizations, the resultant need to exchange data for the growing range of applications, sharing of files, storage, and peripheral devices became apparent. The proliferation of personal computers, such as the IBM PC, and the eventual networking of increased numbers of users (from clerks to executives), has driven the evolution of data communications. Computer-to-computer, as well as terminal-to-computer, communications became necessary.

As a result, data communications not only changed, but accelerated. The distributed processing network and the associated data communications network gained more processing power collectively, more than was possible for a large central computer to manage alone. Users gained the economies and efficiencies made possible through accessing and sharing valuable distributed resources, equipment, computational power, databases, and specialized software.

In many cases, this process enveloped both data and voice networks. Previously, voice communications was analog while data communications was digital, making them distinctly separate (see Glossary for *analog* and *digital*). Now voice is being digitized and data communications has become a complex issue. There is no longer a clear distinction between data and voice. Those facilities originally developed for voice now carry both voice and data, and vice versa. With each passing day, it becomes harder to differentiate between digitized data, voice, facsimile, video, and so forth. Information moving from one point to another has become one continuous stream of digital data.

Due to this movement of information in digital data form, and given the importance of information to the corporation, data communications is now a vital component of a corporation's tele-communications needs. Hence a rapid proliferation of data devices is anticipated, especially from 1985 to 1990. The current rapid increase of demand for remote terminals (CRTs, printers, etc.) indicates that data transmission facilities and networking methods must be developed in the intelligent building. Integrated voice/data PBXs and local area networks may initially fulfill this role. But as data transmission needs grow, a data PBX may be required.

The primary motivation for using a data PBX is cost. The price of a data line on the current generation integrated voice/data PBX systems is running $800 to $1,000, while a data PBX line is available for as little as $150. The solution to increased data switching needs is not using up expensive voice ports on a voice/data PBX, but adding a data PBX to the building information system.

Most corporations project that data services will double by 1990, raising the prospect of spillover of switched data traffic into the telephone system. A voice/data PBX can efficiently handle this load up to a 10 percent capacity without additional processing capability. Beyond that point it is more efficient to add a data PBX. Data PBXs will play an increasingly important role in intelligent buildings because it is predicted that by 1988, data will account for over 30 percent of all PBX traffic.

LOCAL AREA NETWORKS AND OTHER TRANSMISSION MEDIUMS

A local area network (LAN) is a hardware/software system that provides connections for voice and data communications. LANs provide reliable, cost-efficient, high-speed interconnections for compatible and, in some cases, incompatible computers and terminals. They enable devices from many different manufacturers to communicate freely with each other, without regard to individual differences (see Figure 5–6).

LANs serve as the major means of transmitting information among the various equipment indigenous to an intelligent building: personal workstations, microprocessors, microfiles, databases, and interactive graphics-producing systems (see Figure 5–7). By emphasizing a systems rather than component-by-component approach, LANs can dramatically increase user productiv-

FIGURE 5–6 The LAN Ties the Office Together

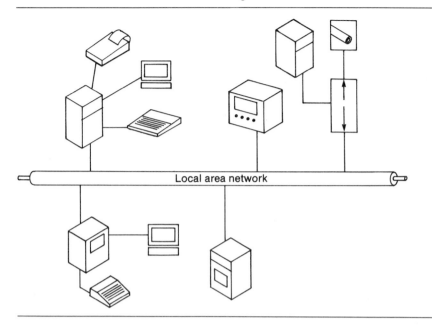

Local area network

FIGURE 5–7 The LAN Ties the Building Together

ity to accommodate an organization's changing goals and structure.

LAN Services and Features

While LAN features may differ according to the software employed, they generally offer:

- Electronic mail message service.
- Data and text transmission.
- Graphics handling and transmission.
- External database access.
- Optical character reader (OCR) input.
- Printer output.
- Editable document transfer.
- Laser video disk.
- Video teleconferencing.
- Network security.
- Network management statistics.

LAN capabilities meet tenants' and facility managers' increasing need to communicate information. Data and text transmission serve not only the automated office but also the microprocessors responsible for sending a continual stream of information to building systems that manage and control energy, and fire and life safety. They are the neural system of the command and control center, responsible for guaranteeing that a building functions intelligently. The LAN and its wiring determine the degree to which a building is truly intelligent.

Defining Characteristics of a LAN

There is still considerable debate over just what a local area network is. Definitions are as diverse as the number of products available. Generally, a LAN, like a PBX, is owned or used exclusively by a single organization, is geographically limited in its use (local), and contains some form of switching technology. The prime distinguishing characteristic is that a LAN contains a much faster transmission rate than either a switch or an external network that covers a broader geographic area.

Today there are over 20 major LAN suppliers and a growing list of minor ones. Few of their products are compatible. For example, almost every LAN has its own proprietary signaling or access technique. (While there is a growing body of international standards, the existing base of dissimilar LANs and lack of vendor support of standards create problems of incompatibility.)

Another distinguishing LAN characteristic is that it uses a single cable, most often coaxial, to carry a tremendous quantity of data. Devices connect directly to the cable, or more typically, to branches that tap off the main cable. These connections are accomplished by breaking data streams into packets, which bear the address of both the sending and receiving devices. Thousands of devices can share the same cable, and because the intelligence is distributed among independent devices, no single failure can bring down the network. LANs are virtually error-free, having powerful error-checking and automatic-correction capabilities built into the networks.

Sending information in packets (analogous to a train boxcar), termed *packet switching*, differentiates LANs from PBXs. Many LANs use packet switching to achieve high performance through shared access to a single cable. Packet switching is a relatively new form of digital communication in which data bits are grouped into bursts (or packets) of fixed length that enables them to share a channel with other packets. When received at the destination, these bursts are separated and sent to the appropriate recipients.

LANs are effective for packet transmission because users tend to send short transmissions of large amounts of data separated by long periods in which relatively little data is sent. Peak data rates are much higher than average data rates. LANs take advantage of this characteristic; they use capacity only when they need it. Packets from many nodes can be intermixed on the cable, giving each node the ability to transmit at up to the full link rate—typically 1 to 10 Mbps or more—when necessary. These higher rates are becoming increasingly desirable.

Both office automation and data processing require more intelligent workstations to transmit and share files and programs with each other as well as with distributed hosts. The increasing use of graphics also requires higher transmission speeds.

Intelligent buildings, with integrated voice and data networks, benefit greatly from the speed and reliability of LANs. They play an important role not only in automating the office, but also in providing security, data communications, and fire and safety networks. LANs act as an intelligent building's major arteries.

LAN Designs

LAN design differences are based on the topology, access signaling technique, and transmission medium chosen by the manufacturer.

Topology. There are various ways to interconnect workstations on local area networks. The physical layouts, or topologies, have three common configurations:

- Bus.
- Ring.
- Star (See Figure 5-8).

The bus LAN. Many consider this topology to be the easiest system to install. It comprises a single cable, often running in linear fashion from one office to a distant location where the cable terminates. Each workstation along the cable taps into the cable to gain network access. A failure of one node in a bus network brings only that particular node down and does not affect the rest of the network, since each station is hooked onto the network in a multilocation manner. Although limitations of cable length and number of nodes exist—depending on the given network—a node can tap into the cable at any given point.

There is no doubt that bus networks have the highest reliabil-

FIGURE 5-8 LAN Topologies

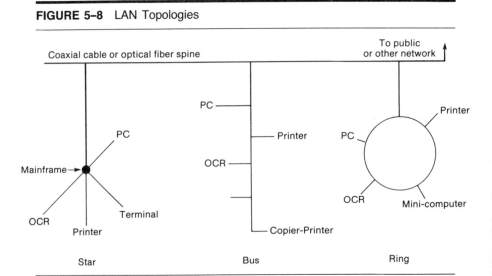

Star　　　　　　　　　　　Bus　　　　　　　　　Ring

ity of all three LAN topologies, although this comes within a limited performance range. However, this is true only for the short length of a single bus segment where no repeaters are necessary. In the XEROX Ethernet(R) LAN, for example, that segment length is 500 meters, beyond which a repeater must be inserted in the network's line or backbone. This changes the reliability picture. A stuck or a short-circuited repeater can render a network unusable. As LANs must serve an entire intelligent building, they necessarily extend beyond 500 meters.

The ring LAN. As the name implies, workstations on this type of LAN are connected in a physical ring. Information is passed circularly until it is captured. A ring LAN only differs from the bus approach in that the last workstation must return the information flow to the first station to repeat the loop. In a ring network, the point-to-point links between stations on the ring simplify network design and eliminate multidrop bus reliability problems. Like a bus, however, rings have repeaters on the line which pose the same potential reliability problems.

One problem with the ring topology is that the entire ring fails if one workstation is turned off or "crashes." This problem can be alleviated by building a bypass relay in the workstation. This closes the station when power is removed and reroutes the signal.

The star LAN. The star (or cluster) system uses a hub approach. Each workstation is connected directly to the hub (central computer), much like the spokes of a wheel. The least flexible LAN topology, it restricts the number of nodes and placement of such peripherals as printers. This limits networking benefits.

Access signaling techniques. There are also a number of access signaling techniques available for communicating on either baseband or broadband LANs. They can all be broadly classified as either polling or contention techniques.

Polling Techniques. Polling techniques determine the order in which nodes take turns accessing the network. One polling technique is token-passing. It is synchronous and occurs in real time. A token is a specially marked, empty data packet that is passed from node to node around a physical loop. When a node wants to transmit, it waits for the token and replaces it with data packets. The recipient puts the token back on the loop when the message has been received.

Contention techniques. Contention techniques are asynchronous. That is, each workstation transmits whenever it has something to send and the cable is free of traffic. When a node wants to send a message, the network interface electronics contained in the user's computer checks to see if there is any traffic on the LAN cable. If the cable is busy, the node simply waits. When the cable is clear, a message can be transmitted. Contention techniques anticipate there will be conflicts or collisions of information entered at the same time, and actually uses them to access a common channel.

When one considers the options available, it is clear that the token-passing ring network has much to offer. It is very versatile and satisfies baseband and broadband coaxial cable as well as fiber-optic cable requirements. When token-passing is used on a bus topology, however, performance suffers. A bus network is less efficient than a token-ring network for heavily loaded systems, and has a greater delay under light loads as well. A token-ring network, on the other hand, is less sensitive to network loads. On the bus, the token has a predetermined address or node for each transmission. On the ring network, however, a free token is circulated on the network until it is captured by a node.

Of all the possible LAN architectures, token-passing ring LANs offer the greatest amount of versatility and communications support. In the case of an intelligent building, the tenants and their needs will often change. This is an extremely important consideration in designing a building information network, and the major reason for the concern with flexibility.

Transmission mediums. One of the most controversial issues concerning LANs is which transmission method to use. To a large extent, wiring systems determine the capabilities of a LAN itself, from its cost to technical consideration of speed, distance, and modulation technique.

A building developer may take several different approaches in providing high-speed transmission of voice and data for the multitude of information equipment indigenous to an intelligent building. The three major transmission mediums are:

- Twisted pair.
- Coaxial cable.
- Fiber optics.

Even when switching components are not built in, they act to network separate systems and devices.

Twisted pair. Twisted pair is the most commonly used transmission cabling available today, primarily because it was the only economical technology available until the mid- to late-1970s.

Anyone who has hooked up a stereo set can install a twisted-pair network. The wire is designed to meet all building codes and does not need a conduit. Because it is the least expensive of all mediums for short distances, cost-effective, and easy to install, twisted-pair offers an immediate networking solution for many users. It is still the preferred choice for interior building wiring and short-distance distribution. And when properly conditioned, twisted pair can transmit data at speeds higher than 2.5 Mbps. Most corporate buildings are presently wired with twisted-pair cable.

Coaxial cable. Although the cost of coaxial cable is higher than twisted-pair wire, it is an attractive medium for voice and data integration and provides greater versatility for data transmission. Coaxial cable may be either baseband or broadband. Baseband transmits the basic digital information stream directly into the coax cable. Broadband techniques send the digital information in a modulated wave form using radio frequency carrier or frequency (see Appendix J for discussion on broadband).

When looking at the issue of functionality, there are two reasons that coax-based systems have the advantage over twisted-pair in certain instances. Most coax-based LANs use packet-switching methods. These systems generally employ either broadband or baseband transmission techniques. Packet switching gives network planners the ability to provide services such as error-free communications, which involves complicated error detection and correction methods.

Due to its greater bandwidth, coaxial cable networks (particularly broadband LANs) also allow for multiple communications of video and voice, in addition to data. Twisted-pair systems can carry only voice and data.

Fiber-optic cable. The idea of fiber-optic cable dates back to 1966, but it was not until 1977 that prototype fiber-optic trunks were used to carry line telephone traffic for the Bell System. Fiber-optic cable, like microwave, is presently used as a heavy trunk cable serving equipment such as central offices with high calling rates. However, significant technological advances have been made during the mid-1980s, and the use of fiber optics for local distribution and increased data application is becoming a reality.

Optical fibers are hair-thin strands of glass that transmit information by light pulses (see Figure 5–9). These light pulses become a computer code. A pulse of light is translated as a "one" and no light is recorded as a "zero."

Fiber optics offer advantages in many areas over other transmission mediums:

- Electrical isolation. Fiber-optic cables never short-circuit, shock, or spark. This eliminates the risk of fire hazards.

FIGURE 5–9 Fiber Optic Cable

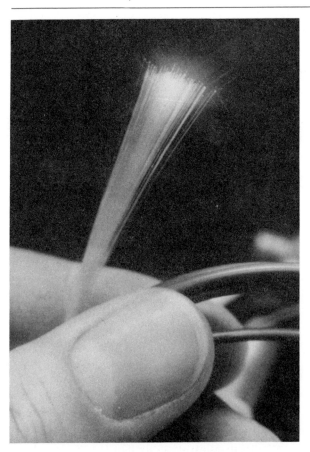

Fiber optics are hair-thin strands of glass which transmit information made up of millions of light pulses per second. They can carry much more information over greater distances than conventional wires.

Photo courtesy of United Technologies Building Systems Company.

Fiber-optic systems are dielectric. Since conductive ties do not exist between areas of different potential, ground loops are completely avoided.

- Wide bandwidth. Optical fibers provide a larger information and traffic-carrying capacity than comparable coaxial cables. This wide bandwidth capability allows higher data rates per given length of cable.
- Low wavelength. Because of its short wavelength, light can carry about 1000 times more information than present electrical communications. A single thin glass fiber can handle up to 240,000 telephone calls and do so without electromagnetic interference.
- Low attenuation. Because of the purity of the glass, optical fibers offer lower signal attenuation than coaxial cables, allowing longer transmission distances at high data rates.
- Immunity to electromagnetic interference (EMI) and radio frequency interference (RFI). Optical transmission cables neither pick up nor emit electromagnetic radiation. There are no spurious signals, noise, or cross talk. This immunity is vital in protecting against data distribution errors in telecommunications and computer systems.
- Light weight and small diameter. Weight savings of up to 80 percent can be expected when optical fibers are used for the same transmission capacity as comparable electrical cables. Savings will also be realized because fiber-optic systems can transmit over longer distances without repeaters, need less installed equipment, and can be combined with power cables when available conduit space is limited.
- Secure communications. While fiber-optic systems can be tapped, it is easier to detect intrusion on fiber-optic networks than on other types of networks. Most tapping techniques depend on the existence of an electromagnetic field generated by an electrical signal. A fiber-optic system requires a physical tap, resulting in an easily detectable signal loss.
- Physical strength. Strength-to-weight ratios of optical-fiber cables are much greater than most metal cables.
- Meets present and future requirements. Glass fibers can carry a tremendous amount of digital information—voice, data, and pictures—at a modest cost. Because of fiber's great capacity, new communications hardware can be added to the data highway without the need for much additional wiring.

This allows for future upgrading and growth with the expansion of the microelectronics revolution at a low cost.

• Cost effectiveness. Fiber-optic cables offer savings in purchase and installation costs because they require fewer cables (as full bandwidth capabilities are realized). They also use existing power trays, rather than requiring installation of additional signal conduits.

The capacity for fiber-optic cable expansion is especially important in multitenant intelligent buildings, given the developer's need to build systems that save money and provide for future flexibility. Fiber optics, a powerful new product of the information age, is helping to make buildings smart. Intelligent buildings can use a major artery composed of fiber-optic cable in place of the usual snarl of wires.

Mixed-Media Networks

A misconception about LANs is that once a network is in position, an organization/building must live with it. A variety of LANs are now on the market, offering users multiple solutions—including the option of mixing and matching networks. An important point is that various networks can be linked together. The technology exists, and it is improving.

There is also growing acceptance of the mixed-media approach in which an organization is free to choose the network that suits its needs, with all sub-networks within a facility joined to that central backbone. In this way, each department (or tenant) maintains its autonomy, yet access to central databases and interdepartmental communications is assured.

An example of a mixed-media approach to networking is to use broadband coaxial cable or optical fiber as the media backbone throughout the building, then to install baseband, twisted-pair cable as the ribs that serve individual groups of users/tenants.

With the move toward a mixed-media approach, users do not need to worry about choosing the wrong LAN. The LAN approach provides a flexible, easily expandable system that lets the user configure his or her system as needed. There is no need to commit to broadband over baseband, or twisted-pair over coaxial cable. Rather, users should pick a LAN that provides the most cost-effective solution for their application. When needs change, users can mix and match technologies (see Appendix K for discussion of gateways and standards).

SHORT- AND LONG-HAUL NETWORKS

To fully realize the benefits of an intelligent building, provisions must be made for extra-building communications. These communications may involve only a short distance, termed *short-haul*, or distances over 10 miles, termed *long-haul*. Telephone calls in the same city, transfer of data from telecommuters to the home office, and video teleconferencing between intelligent buildings all require some type of network.

Short-Haul Networks

Short-haul transmission is a practical, cost-effective solution for transmitting voice and/or data up to 10 miles. Short-haul communications generally apply to intra-city (in and around city) transmissions. There are many methods of short-haul transmission, including LANs, twisted pair, coaxial cable, and fiber-optic cable (discussed previously), microwave and light link systems.

While short-haul can be achieved by leasing local telephone company lines (typically twisted copper pair), there are benefits for buildings that provide their own short-haul networks to tenants. The two most important benefits are cost and availability. Leased lines are expensive, if and when they are available.

Microwave. Microwave radio is a popular transmission medium that is most effective when two locations are within line of sight. Many vendors offer cost-justified systems that do not incur monthly telephone charges to connect telephone systems or data systems. In the face of expected mileage charges increases from the local telephone company, microwave might become an attractive alternative for future cost reductions.

Microwave is primarily used for point-to-point, line-of-sight transmission and requires expensive equipment at each end, in addition to the twisted pair still necessary for local distribution. However, microwave can be connected directly to the latest PBXs, facilitating the linkage of intelligent buildings to teleports (see Figure 5–10). LANs can also be connected via short-haul microwave link, providing such services as electronic mail, facsimile, and digitized video teleconferencing.

The distance of microwave transmission is dependent on five factors:

- The amount of up time required—the high standard is 99.995 percent, or 26 minutes a year of down time.

FIGURE 5–10 Typical Microwave Linkage

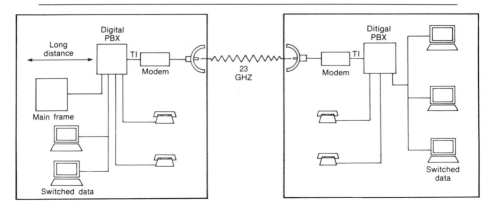

Microwave links intelligent buildings together.

- Local rainfall—a well-engineered microwave path may not be extremely sensitive to rainfall, although outages may occur in some cases.
- Terrain—microwave is line-of-sight, so that bypassing mountains and other interference requires repeaters.
- Size of the antenna and the performance of the radio.
- Data rate speed.

Typically, paths in the 23 gigahertz (GHz) range of the frequency spectrum are from 1 to 10 miles long.

On the issue of security, microwave transmissions can be tapped. However, microwave transmission has a very narrow bandwidth which is difficult to home in on. In addition, scramblers can be built in, providing effective encryption protection. It is important to note that microwave transmission may be considerably more secure than traditional telephone use.

A license to operate a private microwave system must be obtained for implementing microwave service. Then buildings can be linked to connect PBXs or transmit data. Although a frequency must be found which nobody else is using, this is not as yet difficult. Unlike the lower frequency banks, 23 GHz is relatively uncrowded and easy to coordinate.

Light link (infrared).   Light link is the use of infrared light waves to link communication between two locations separated by a short distance. Light link will find a niche as a cost effective communications tool because both installing cable and ongoing monthly telephone charges for other systems are not cost effective.

Light link can generally provide a few high-speed communication channels of up to five miles. The limiting factor is poor weather conditions which can inhibit transmission.

Long-Haul Networks

For transmission needs of more than 10 miles, long-haul networks are required. They utilize previously discussed twisted-pair, coaxial, and fiber-optic cable. In addition, they include evolving satellite technology in linking networks over long distances.

Satellites. Satellites offer a cost effective method of long-distance transmission. They provide an alternative means of transmission between two physically separated locations, such as between intelligent buildings or between an intelligent building and a remote site. The speeds available for satellite transmission are well into the hundreds of millions of bits per second, so that satellite channels are typically used for full-color video links or for connection of international telephone conversations. Satellite links become cost effective when the distance to be spanned is over 500 miles, at which point a tremendous bandwidth is obtained at reasonable rates. The distance at which using the technology becomes cost effective is decreasing as technology evolves.

While satellites may play an important role in linking intelligent buildings or in simply supplying long-distance interconnection to people in an intelligent building, they have some drawbacks. One is their inherent delay due to the distances they span. Even at the speed of light, it takes a half-second for a message to travel from the earth to the satellite and return. While these delays are noticeable during telephone conversations, they typically do not have major impact on voice communications. Most executives do not like to talk over satellites because of this annoying delay, however. These same delays can cause major problems during data transmission if specific action is not taken to compensate for the delays in data acknowledgments.

Another factor is the expense of installing an earth dish on the roof of an intelligent building. Satellite transmission facilities have become less expensive. As higher powered satellites are used and smaller ground stations are employed, a new form of satellite communications, called direct broadcast system (DBS), has emerged. DBS uses more expensive, high-powered satellites, but allows for smaller, very low-cost earth receivers (about the size of a trash can lid). It is in the area of DBS that most future satellite applications will emerge.

This particular method of transmission provides excellent digital voice and data transmission. Unfortunately, the technology is only economical when used on high-density links. The cost of satellite transmission facilities makes it an ineffective method for local service. DBS has also proven to be a very competitive substitute for local distribution systems in which a heavy amount of traffic to remote areas exists. The supply of voice telephone and data services from the building PBX to portable (and, in some cases, fixed) terminals in remote areas provides connections for people working outside the main office. Voice and data communication is uninterrupted.

As the number of intelligent buildings increases, an international business communications network may be created by linking them. Advances in satellite-related technology will make much of this interconnection possible.

A truly smart building is one which has automated everything.

Automated Building-Control Systems

INTRODUCTION

Intelligent buildings are the blending of two separate technologies: building automation and information technology. This chapter covers building automation systems. These include:

- Energy management and control systems.
- Security systems.
- Life support systems.

ENERGY MANAGEMENT AND CONTROL SYSTEMS (EMCS)

Energy and building operations are controllable costs that can be simplified in the intelligent building. They are the most significant factors for improving the balance sheet and enhancing the market edge in today's highly competitive building market. Energy costs represent a substantial portion of overall operating expenses (more than one third of the total). Proper energy management offers one of the most direct ways to effect savings in building operations.[1]

The efficiency and reliability of the mechanical/electrical systems of any facility also determine both costs and the ability to provide comfortable conditions or production support. As the costs of energy and labor rise, the importance of optimum system selection, design, and construction increases. Energy management is therefore an increasingly important function of any building.

How Does an EMCS Work?

An EMCS uses a computer with simple or elaborate programs that override "local loop" controls under specific conditions, and thus conserve more energy than the controls would alone (see Figure 6–1). *Local loop* refers to those controls that directly relate, and are usually contiguous, to a single heating, ventilating, and air conditioning (HVAC) system.

The HVAC itself is an important consideration in the intelligent building that is filled with automated office equipment. It is therefore important to consider expandable HVAC systems. As an office approaches a one-to-one ratio of people to terminals, an additional 1 to 1.2 devices for every terminal can be expected. These additional devices are printers, copy machines, distributing processing units, and so on, which also generate additional heat. Terminals produce as much heat as 1 to 1.5 people doing work,

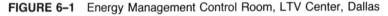

FIGURE 6–1   Energy Management Control Room, LTV Center, Dallas

Photo courtesy of United Technologies Building Systems Company.

sitting still. This ratio of people to terminals means a more than doubled apparent occupancy of a building.

Today's interior office designs call for a mix between the open plan approach and enclosed spaces. A good variety of HVAC zoning to handle these variations prevents getting locked in or out of planning options. This flexibility is extremely important. It is also important to consider the possible concentration of electronic hardware in one location. Cooling of that area will need to be increased, but if equipment is distributed evenly throughout all

FIGURE 6–2   The Energy Communications Service Adjunct

Automating the entire building.

areas, all cooling must be increased. An EMCS can handle these necessary variations of temperature.

An energy management control system can be as simple as a time clock, or as complex as a computer-based system with elaborate monitoring and control hardware and software. It is this latter computer-based system that an intelligent building uses to manage energy. It is possible for it to also include other functions such as maintenance scheduling, fire and smoke control, security, and the reporting associated with all of these (see Figure 6–2).

The Primary Functions of an EMCS

Among the many functions that energy management and control system manufacturers offer in their individual systems, the most important are:

- Monitoring.
- Programming.
- Control.
- Graphics.
- Alarms.
- Logging.

Monitoring. Items to be monitored comprise such things as overall temperature, boiler operation, pump status, sump pump levels, and critical area temperatures (required in computer rooms). Monitoring for optimal operation includes outdoor air quality, exterior and interior zone temperatures, electrical demand, and prime water temperatures and flows.

Programming. Equipment may be programmed to turn on or off automatically, as needed. The key is to determine when and for how long it can remain off without adversely affecting tenants or the building equipment operations. A properly programmed EMCS with sufficient sensors and function, such as optimum time to start system functions, provides this type of time cycle and load-demand control.

Control. Direct control, or intervention, of the local loop is necessary to the usefulness of the EMCS. Intervention due to fluctuations or disturbances outside normal parameters helps to return the system to optimum efficiency. Intervention control

FIGURE 6–3

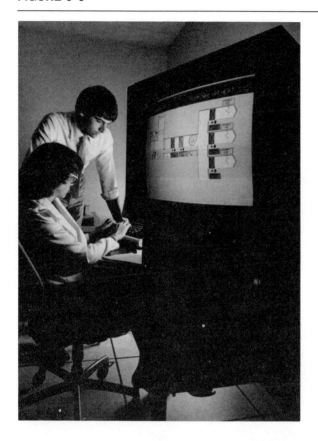

Building automation is one aspect of a building's intelligence, providing centralized control of heating, ventilating and air conditioning. This system, in the Tabor Center, Denver, also monitors and controls elevators, lighting, fire and security, and electronic office services.

Photo courtesy of United Technologies Building Systems Company.

primarily includes start-stop of motors and reset of local-loop controller set points (see Figure 6–3).

Graphics.   Full-color graphic representations of air handling systems, pumping loops, process systems, building outlines, smoke zones, fire-alarm zones, site plans, and graphs are available with most large systems. Graphic displays of measured variables aid the operator in understanding the systems and are particularly valuable in training new operators.

Alarms. Critical points on the network should be connected to an alarm program. Most monitoring systems provide easily set high and low alarm limits for each point. If the measured value exceeds a limit in either direction, the operator is alerted to correct the situation. This function often includes fire, smoke, and security alarms.

Logging. The ability to print out a permanent record of variables and alarms is a feature of an increasing number of EMCSs. Printers can be programmed to print out specific variables at specified times, to print alarms whenever they occur, to record the time alarmed conditions return to normal, or any variation of the above. Preventive maintenance work orders and reports can also be printed out if a suitable program is incorporated into the system. In the long run, historical data and analyses are most useful for improving system operation.

Benefits of an EMCS

The function of the EMCS is to improve existing or new system operations by analyzing all the interacting factors of building use and environmental needs. The EMCS conserves energy while maintaining satisfactory building environment control. The ultimate EMCS benefit is, of course, lowered energy costs. An EMCS can also contribute to cost reduction in other ways, such as providing greater safety and better maintenance (See Table 6–1).

An EMCS also adjusts the building systems for more efficient, accurate operation. For example, heating and air conditioning systems have sensors that pick up environmental changes (such as the sun shining on one part of a building), and adjust temperatures automatically. Sensors on each floor monitor, and com-

---

Table 6–1 Benefits of an EMCS

Low operating cost of EMCS:

- Energy savings—Equipment is continually controlled and optimized to operate at peak efficiency.
- Labor savings—Productivity of the labor force is enhanced by consolidating control under a single system.
- Maintenance savings—Failures and excessive wear of plant equipment can be reduced with automated maintenance scheduling.

puters adjust, airflow and temperature. This is extremely important, given the expected ratio of one person to one terminal in the near future. The benefits are both in economics and ergonomics, and labor and maintenance costs can be reduced. Failures and excessive wear of plant equipment can also be reduced with automated maintenance scheduling.

BUILDING SECURITY SYSTEMS

Automated building security systems, like energy management systems, have been used in more traditionally designed buildings for some time. Their novelty in the intelligent building lies not in their inclusion, but in their degree of automation, and the extent to which they are interconnected with other building systems. This point will be covered in the following chapter, but a brief description of security systems is presented here.

Security systems provide three types of protection by monitoring connected security sensors:

- Perimeter protection.
- Area protection.
- Object protection.

They are used to control access to a building or restricted area by authorized personnel. Such people are identified through the use of magnetic card readers, card keys, or other access identification devices. At this point, the system opens the proper door to allow entry to, or exit from, the restricted area.

Should unauthorized entrance be obtained, some systems not only provide printed reports and visual displays of break-ins, but also follow the intruder's progress throughout the building on a color graphics monitor. This function is included in only the most sophisticated security systems on the market, and requires extensive wiring to support the necessary sensors. Installation of such systems is simplified by an abundantly wired intelligent building.

NETWORK LIFE-SUPPORT SYSTEMS

A network life-support system is needed to ensure smooth operation once the network has been fully configured and is running. When this system is tied into the building information network, it provides the power and environmental conditions which guarantee the continual functioning of the building information systems.

Though made of silicon and steel, PBXs and computers require a life-support system and a highly specific physical environment to ensure their proper functioning. In the case of a power outage and resultant shutdown of the PBX alone, companies can lose tens of thousands of dollars in business. The developer of an intelligent building cannot afford to ignore the need for a secure information-systems environment for his or her tenants and equipment. Although initial investments are large, they cost less than a single computer disaster.

The components of a network life-support system are:

- Uninterrupted power supply (UPS).
- Power conditioners.
- Air conditioning.

Uninterrupted Power Supply

The UPS is designed to feed emergency electricity to the components of an information network and air conditioners in the event of municipal power failure. In the critical first moments of a blackout, UPS batteries automatically send power to the computer system. The life span of these batteries is from two to eight hours, enough time to save existing data and shut down the system or verify that a back up diesel generator will supply power without mechanical failure.

The costs of UPS, other than the initial capital investment and ongoing maintenance, are for storage and related battery needs. The practical issue of safely housing the batteries and diesel generator must be addressed, since fumes from batteries are toxic, and fuel for the diesel generator is volatile. The generator and storage tanks must be stored in a protected and secure area, such as an isolated structure at a distance from populated areas or the basement of a city high-rise building. Because only maintenance personnel need physical access to the UPS, inconvenient locations are adequate in all respects. It should be noted that other personnel need access to the UPS test switch. This switch should be activated at least once a week to ensure the system functions properly.

Power Conditioners

Power conditioners are the "pacemakers" of the UPS. They constantly adjust the energy flow, keeping voltage within 3 or 4 percent of a specified level. This conditioning is critical, since fluctuation of municipal power systems is often 5 to 7 percent. Even greater variances occur in midsummer when air conditioning plays havoc with municipal power. This is important because fluctuations add wear and tear to the switch and computers, can cause disturbances in data flows, and can even result in data distortion.

AC power-line disturbances (blackouts) occur less frequently than sags (decreases in power-line voltage), impulses (short-term overvoltages), and surges. These sags, impulses, or surges actually cause more damage in the long run than power failures. They cause information erasures and premature equipment burnout, which are potentially expensive to businesses relying on clean data flows.

Intelligent buildings, therefore, need power conditioning first and foremost. Most UPS systems do not address high-voltage transient problems. Power conditioners protect hardware and generally reside in the computer room, where operators can use the machine's monitoring and self-test features frequently. The electrical source for mechanical systems need not be serviced by the operators, but it should be tied into the UPS system.

Air Conditioning

Computers are as sensitive to changes in temperature and humidity as they are to jumps and drops in power. Their needs outstrip the capacity of standard air conditioning systems for three reasons:

- Computers operate within a plus or minus 2 degree temperature range, with a relative humidity range of plus or minus 5 percent (generally around 72 degrees Fahrenheit and 50 percent RH). Many standard air conditioning systems cannot maintain an environment within these parameters.
- The standard air conditioning system of the average building is controlled seasonally (May 1 through October 1) and daily (8 AM to 6 PM). Computers, however, operate 24 hours a day year round, constantly generating heat and creating the need for constant, autonomous cooling.
- Since the same city power systems that are prone to blackout also drive the air conditioners which cool the computers,

companies should consider linking air conditioning systems into a UPS system for back up purposes.

Like UPS systems, air conditioning compressors may be located outside the computer room. Only maintenance personnel need access to them. But because air conditioning functions constantly and is a mechanical system, it must occasionally be shut down for repairs. Computer systems cannot tolerate this loss, so standby air conditioning must be available.

Computer rooms should be located in the interior of a building, away from outside windows so the air conditioning system does not have to battle heat gain from summer sun coming through windows or onto the roof. This means the least desirable spaces for people are perfectly appropriate for use as vaults for these sensitive machines.

Air conditioned air is usually distributed under the same raised floor that accommodates computer wiring. The facilities manager needs to examine all new and changed wiring plans to confirm that cables will not block airflow in the 12- or 18-inch space below the raised floor.

Evolving networks, switches, and the computers they connect require environments that are more, not less, specific. Advanced computers require a super-cooled environment, far beyond simple air conditioning. If tenants expect to keep up with the changing work environment, they need to look ahead and prepare for the technical problems that come with advances. One way of protecting equipment is by choosing an intelligent building that contains on-line power management systems. These protect not only the building information network but also the individual components of the automated office.

CHAPTER SEVEN

In order to maintain management effectiveness and increase organizational efficiency, organizations must plan to integrate all office automation technologies.
The Office Automation Primer
Carolyn Mullins & Thomas West
Prentice Hall, 1982

Information Networking Architectures: Integrating the Technologies

INTRODUCTION

The intelligent building not only incorporates a myriad of devices necessary for the operation of separate building information systems but also links them together for effective use. Such linking creates an information network (see Figures 7–1 and 7–2).

The word *architecture* has acquired a new meaning. In its new context, architecture refers to the mode in which various technologies are employed and integrated to form an information network, which then provides the benefits of data, video, and voice communications, according to Gordon J. Lorig, Jr., district manager for the Advanced Communications Resource Group of the AT&T Resource Management Corporation.[1] To this list, the benefits of building automation may be added.

Many information system architectures are possible; the choice made depends on individual preference, needs, technology, and available funds. The major differences in information network architectures lie in the degree to which functions are integrated or interconnected. This chapter examines the methods of networking that can be incorporated into an intelligent building.

WHAT IS AN INFORMATION NETWORK?

An information network provides for the transmission of signs, signals, images, or sounds by wire, radio, lightwaves, or other

115

FIGURE 7-1 Before Systems Integration

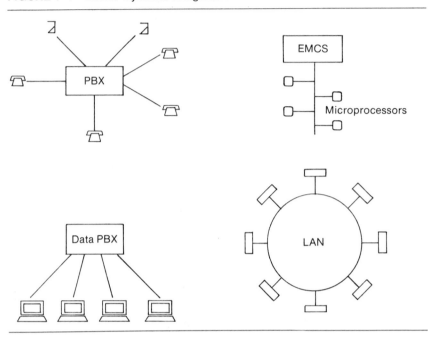

electromagnetic means. An information network allows communications devices to "talk" (interact) with each other on a switched or dedicated basis (allowing any user to be connected to any other user) and to share facilities in order to reduce cost.

Information network equipment may be divided into two categories: (1) equipment used at the individual level in communicating, such as personal computers, and (2) the systems which link them and their peripherals.

Two major technical considerations of an information network should be addressed:

- Existing and future integrated/interconnected transmission facilities.
- Compatibility or need to make dialogue possible between terminals that "speak" different languages.

Integration refers to merging separate systems. There are two types of integration:

- *Physical integration:* Permits voice, data, and video to share the same distribution and switching paths. In addition, data

FIGURE 7-2   After Systems Integration

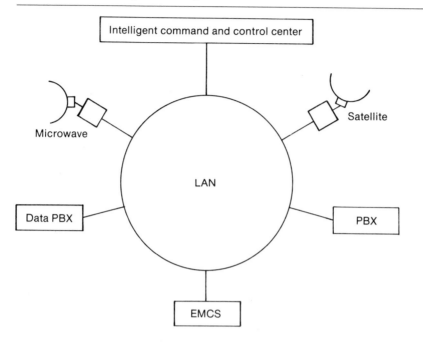

The information network.

interfaces can be physically integrated into the terminal, workstation, or personal computer. The net benefit of physical integration is cost savings, since the same wiring is used for voice and data transmissions.

- *Functional integration:* Allows the user to have a common interface to the capabilities of both the PBX and the host computer. When this exists, a user's single command can result in a file being displayed electronically and a telephone call being made simultaneously from a workstation. Functional integration provides the opportunity to reduce the overhead associated with using the integrated system. This, in turn, improves productivity—so often cited as the major benefit of OA. (See Appendix E for the features which integrated telephone and computer systems should provide users.)

Interconnection refers to the linkage of separate network systems. Some systems are indeed merging, such as PBXs and LANs, but most are more efficient when functionally separate and linked through a communications medium. The method chosen of linking building information systems is determined both by technological capabilities and owner preference.

WHY IS A NETWORK NECESSARY?

The intelligent building is fully functional only when its systems are completely interconnected. A building's intelligence quotient (BIQ) is determined by its information network, the system on which both shared tenant services and building automation depend.

An intelligent building provides savings to developers in energy, wiring, and management. Building automation systems keep energy expenditures to a minimum by constantly monitoring and adjusting to environmental needs. Wiring costs are cut when these building automation systems share wiring facilities with other building information systems. In addition, the interconnection of systems allows for central building network management, which means quicker problem solving and the associated savings.

The centralized wiring scheme is also very functional for multitenant services. By tieing all information systems together through a central nervous system, communications both inside and outside the building are greatly facilitated. Centralized wiring links automated office equipment and provides access to the outside world through satellite and microwave links. It also extends the benefits of office automation to geographically displaced areas.

Individual tenant office automation systems can access other building systems through a building network which is, in turn, connected through to others. Linking intelligent buildings forms "teleports," which provide a more efficient communications method than tieing together thousands of individual tenant systems.

THE CHOICE: PBX OR CENTREX?

The telephone switch is the heart of the intelligent building and therefore the primary consideration in networking a building. Two options are available for providing a switch: a private branch

FIGURE 7-3   The Basic Choice: PBX versus CENTREX

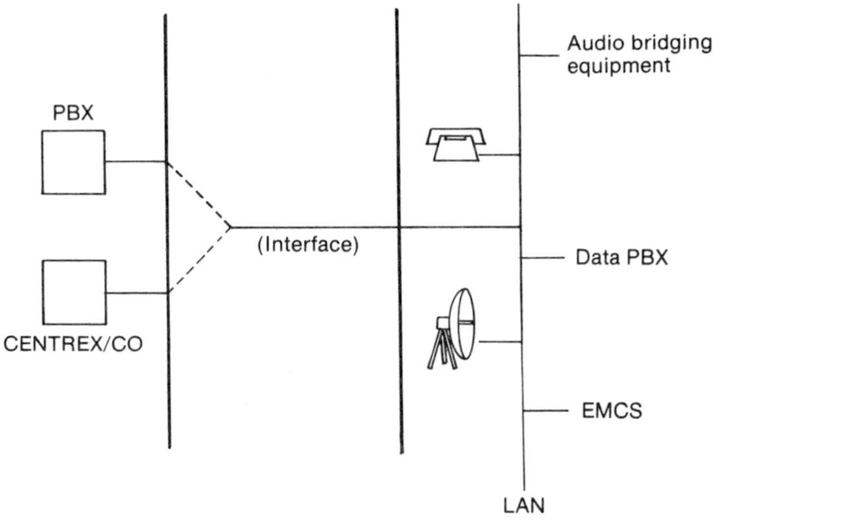

exchange (PBX) on the premises or a central-office-based service, CENTREX (see Figure 7-3).

A comparison of the software functions offered by CEN-TREX and PBXs shows their different capabilities. CENTREX, presently lacking appropriate software, is unable to offer station message detail recording (SMDR) to users.[2] This has become an important service to tenants who believe it will keep skyrocketing telephone costs down. Regulatory issues are responsible for the lack of this feature. While SMDR is not provided on intrastate calls in all states, it is legal in some states for long-distance service. The degree of importance of this service to developers and prospective tenants plays a large part in determining the choice of CENTREX or a PBX.

CENTREX is also limited by not providing queuing or contention functions for switching data. The software of a data PBX provides for the queuing and contention of data. The benefits of CENTREX must be weighed against the costs of adding a data PBX to the intelligent building information system.

CENTREX and PBX interface costs also differ in intelligent building applications. Whether the interface from the building's information network to CENTREX is at the central office or within the building, distance charges must be paid for each trunk.

In cases where an intelligent building is close to its telephone company's central office, these costs may be less than those of a PBX and its maintenance. Hence, distance from a central office may be a determining factor in choosing a switching technology.

Combining both data and voice transmission on the telephone can increase costs for CENTREX users. This currently requires extra wire pairs at every jack, a consideration that makes the task of interconnecting building systems more costly and technically difficult when using CENTREX. However, as more central offices install digital switches, this issue will disappear.

CENTREX vendors, however, argue that space is saved in a high-rent building where it is otherwise dedicated to a PBX and its support systems. The most important support system is an Uninterrupted Power Supply (UPS), which guarantees that in the event of power failure, the telephone system will not be adversely affected. In a fully intelligent building, special space and UPS requirements already exist for the other systems (such as an energy management system).

CENTREX vendors also state that no building manager wants to become a small telephone company. Most would be happy to let the local telephone company oversee management and maintenance of the switch. In an intelligent building, where many systems are most efficiently managed in concert, this argument loses some strength. Increasingly, the trend is toward hiring specialists to oversee the systems so that managers escape becoming a "mini Bell" telephone company but retain control over the system.

Another argument in favor of CENTREX is the absolute dependability of the central-office-based switch. PBXs are presently engineered for a mean time of one month between failures. However, there is a chance that a number of calls will be lost each month through PBX failure. The switches designed for central offices, in contrast, have a mean time of 40 years between failures.[3] For many, this issue is critical.

As software is developed for central offices switches which supports multitenant needs, and these switches are installed in intelligent buildings, this issue will disappear. This software is now being developed for a 1A ESS switch, used in many central offices. In addition, with powerful UPS systems guaranteeing sufficient power, the odds of an intelligent building's switch going down through power failure are extremely small.

Another strong argument for CENTREX is its flexibility. As more intelligent building tenants use the telephone system, lines can be expanded. And as the system is reconfigured to allow data and video applications, it can be further expanded. When rapid expansion of the system is expected, CENTREX can be implemented without major capital expenditures for what could, later, prove to be unnecessary capacity.

While modular PBXs are designed to accommodate expansion, they must be sufficiently large from the outset to meet the expected growth in demand for voice, data, and video transmission. With CENTREX, developers need not invest in capacity that they will not need for years. This flexibility comes at a price, and uncertainty of tenant demand for such applications in the future may make this price too high. CENTREX is a strong alternative to a PBX, although unresolved issues of access charges and services that CENTREX may legally offer cloud the picture.

CENTREX versus PBX—Issues

Developers choosing between PBX and CENTREX systems must be aware of differences in service offerings, such as the following:

ISSUE	CENTREX	PBX
Borrowing requirement*	No	Yes
Initial cost	Low	High
Ongoing cost	Uncertain	Rising
Maintenance		
Response time	Immediate	2–4 hours
Cost	Included	$3–5/set/month
Backup costs	Included	Optional
Space requirements	Little	Expensive
Power requirements	None	Expensive
Multisite capability		
No additional equipment	Yes	No
Features		
Now	Few	Many
Future	More	Many
Cost	High	High
Expandability	Easy	Difficult
Data transmission		
Now	Low speed	High speed
Future	High speed	High speed
Low speed to 9600 BPS		
High speed above 9600 BPS		
SMDR	Per station	Per system
Least-cost routing	No**	Yes
Office automation	No**	Yes
Moves and changes		
Customer controlled	No**	Yes
Cost	Low	High

* Financial capability required to purchase.
** Presently restricted by regulatory authority.

ADDING THE LOCAL AREA NETWORK (LAN)

Intelligent buildings house a large variety of terminals, computers, word processors, and peripherals. These require a network which can support varied needs. Due to speed limitations, some of these needs cannot be met by a switch. LANs have evolved to provide reliable, cost-efficient, high-speed interconnection for incompatible computers and terminals. An in-house PBX and a "telco" (telephone company) based CENTREX service present different methods of interconnecting the very important local area network.

CENTREX/Local Area Network

In intelligent building applications, a major CENTREX failing is that simultaneous voice and data communication over the same cable pair is not yet available. Manufacturers have been working to solve this problem, and systems are now available which provide voice/data integration for CENTREX users. These systems provide an interface between CENTREX and the building's local area network (LAN). This resolves two problems: (1) How a CENTREX service should be interconnected with the LAN and (2) How voice/data integration can be provided.

The interface can be a data PBX (see Chapter Three, Data

FIGURE 7-4 The CENTREX/LAN Interface

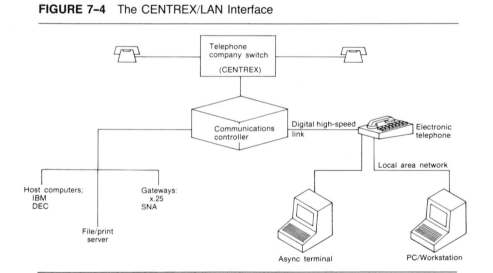

PBX), positioned between the telephone system and the station user, that provides voice and data capability on an integrated basis (see Figure 7-4). Thus, using a single instrument, the user can simultaneously transmit voice and asynchronous data or incorporate a LAN interface into a single telephone instrument. All of this may be done on a single twisted pair.

The choice of CENTREX as the heart of an information network generally requires a data PBX to switch the increasing rate of data traffic entering and leaving the building network. The data PBX, through the LAN, also serves as the interface between CENTREX and all other building information systems. The telephone system is transparent through installation of this interface.

While CENTREX has certain drawbacks, it must be considered a possible system choice because it can be interconnected with a data PBX. Whether it can maintain its viability depends on possible service offerings which regulators are presently debating. Its use will vary depending on applications and relative cost.

PBX/Local Area Network

There has been a heated controversy over which system—modern PBXs or emerging LAN systems—plays the major role in office automation and information networking (see Figure 7-5). Available options for serving those needs include:

- Separate, parallel voice and data networks, with the PBX controlling only voice (see Figure 7-6).
- All office traffic handled over a star-, bus-, or ring-configured local network with a switch as the controller (see Figure 7-7).
- A baseband or broadband LAN interconnected to a PBX-controlled network (see Figure 7-8).

PBX advocates hold that the PBX approach has advantages in terms of installation, ease of voice/data integration, reliability, and cost. LAN advocates emphasize the advantage of a high bandwidth and related very high transmission speeds for applications such as video teleconferencing and computer-to-computer communications. The transmission speed limitations of most third-generation PBXs will not suffice for these.

The only PBX limitation evident from the above comparison is that of available speed and bandwidth provided by the tele-

FIGURE 7-5

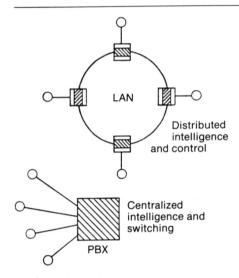

The PBX and the LAN—Two different approaches for interoffice communications.

phone system. In view of this, the PBX is generally accepted as the key to the integrated building information network.

LANs, nonetheless, play an increasingly important part in linking separate network systems within a building. They serve the high-bandwidth devices in an integrated building information system, such as the main computing facilities, the PBX, EMCS and its microprocessors, high-volume print and file servers, and video teleconferencing facilities. While the data handling capability of third-generation PBXs might seem adequate for most intelligent-building needs, current high-powered workstations with high-

FIGURE 7-6 Parallel Systems

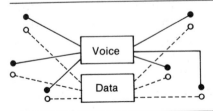

FIGURE 7-7

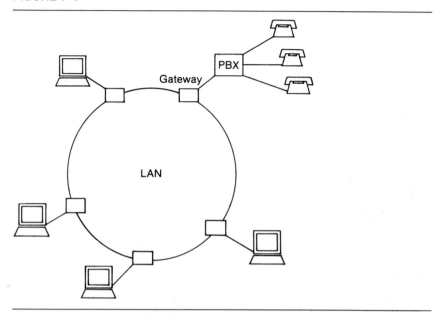

FIGURE 7-8

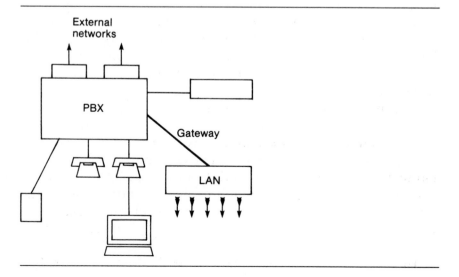

TABLE 7-1 A Comparison of PBX and LAN Characteristics

	PBX	LAN
Characteristics:		
Simplicity	X	X
Lower cost	X	
Flexibility	X	X
Standardized	X	
Speed/bandwidth	1Mbps	300Mbps
(Future)	(10Mbps)	

resolution displays employ even higher data transfer rates, and full-motion video teleconferencing systems also require wide bandwidths.

How high does the data transmission rate have to be in order to satisfy workplace requirements? LAN vendors cite an example of one person at a terminal using an on-screen graphics capability to make business forecasts. Such forecasts require that the screen be filled with large bursts of data at high speed. A second person in the same office is transferring files from one system to another. Both tasks require a large amount of channel capacity and speed to interact meaningfully.

The speed that tenants require will determine the roles the PBX and LAN will play in an intelligent building. While the typical office worker's needs are served by a PBX today, a growing demand for graphics, file transfers, and other functions requiring high speed data rates is expected soon. Other intelligent building services such as full-motion video teleconferencing rooms, also demand the high speeds of a LAN. Intelligent building developers need to be able to offer these attractive services to tenants through the capacity of a LAN.

Enhancements of third-generation PBXs (considered 3.5 or 4th generation), which offer even more sophisticated high-speed data communications capabilities, have blurred the distinctions between PBX and LAN solutions. The current trend in information networking design is for modern PBXs and LANs to coexist and be integrated into an optimum system configuration. This would use PBX switching and LAN transmission capabilities. The issue is not which system to use, but how to interconnect or integrate them.

Integration of voice and data is increasingly viewed by office automation specialists as the most economical and sensible approach to managing office voice and data communications traffic. However, problems of cost-effectiveness, incompatibility of products, and total system reliability emerge when voice and data are managed on separate networks within an office. Furthermore, the separate network approach does not prepare an office for the near-certain "explosion" of voice and data communications traffic in the future. The integrated approach, on the other hand, provides for increased future capacity.

ADDING THE BUILDING AUTOMATION SYSTEMS

An energy management system can be integrated into other building systems, such as the switch or local area network. Automated systems for fire detection, safety, and security can also be integrated with energy management. This overall building automation system is generally referred to as an energy management and control system (EMCS).

Integration of an EMCS

CENTREX and PBXs differ in their capacities to integrate an EMCS into building information networks. Unlike CENTREX, some PBXs are designed to support energy management functions. Energy management is achieved, as are most PBX functions, through software that allows one piece of equipment to

FIGURE 7-9 PBX with Energy Management Software

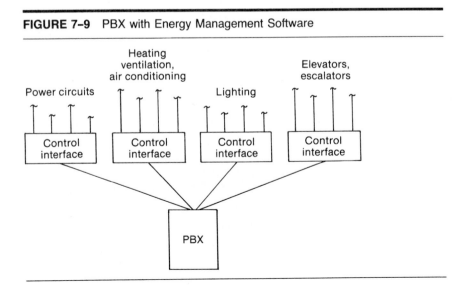

control both telecommunications and building automation functions (see Figure 7–9). However, the quality of an integrated PBX/ EMCS is inferior to that of separate EMCS systems designed by experts in the field. Therefore, the ability to support both functions through one system is not a strong selling point of PBXs over CENTREX.

Either a CENTREX service or PBX may be interconnected with a separate energy management system through the intelligent building's local area network.

EMCS/LAN Interconnection. Why should an HVAC engineer be interested in using a local area network (LAN) designed for communication? "Because it can cut energy monitoring and control system installation costs by 25 percent and cut wiring costs in half," according to James L. Coggins.[4] The wiring between the central computer of an EMCS and the various devices it controls can account for up to half the total installed wiring cost for a building. Using a LAN for the communications link between various parts of the EMCS can help justify the installation of both systems.

An added benefit of using a LAN for transmission is that it is very adaptable. Because all signals are available anywhere on a LAN, and such systems are typically modular in design, new equipment can be added and old equipment moved without running new wire. Consequently, as the ability to monitor a building's functions evolves, new sensing equipment can be added to a LAN as needed. For example, automated devices might be attached that open or close blinds to control solar heating.

The function of the EMCS is to further improve a system's operation through analysis of all the interacting factors of building use, as well as environmental needs. A LAN provides access to all points throughout an intelligent building so that the total building environment can be continuously monitored. An EMCS may function at maximum potential when integrated with a LAN. Paybacks of three years or less is typical of office buildings with a LAN-based EMCS, as opposed to much longer periods for buildings in which the systems are not integrated.[5]

There are many approaches to EMCS data transmission. At one extreme, single computer systems are designed to interface with broadband cable and take advantage of its communications capability. At the other end of the communications spectrum there are units that rely heavily on distributed processing, which minimizes the need for communications. These systems rely on small stand-alone units that are polled periodically by a central computer. The central computer can thus obtain historical data, change set points such as temperature settings, or activate an alarm when appropriate.

Integration of Building Automation Systems

A truly smart building has everything automated, its elevators, heating, cooling, lights, fire safety, and security systems. Why is automation smart? Because it is economical. For example, lighting amounts to 40 percent of an office building's energy consumption. Most people still neglect to turn off the lights when they leave a room. Systems have been developed which manage this problem by automatically turning lights off and on as someone walks into or out of an office. If no movement is detected for 12 minutes, the lights turn off (see Figure 7–10). Savings in this area alone can be significant.

Heating and air-conditioning sensors pick up environmental changes (such as the sun shining on one part of a building) and adjust temperatures automatically. Sensors on each floor monitor airflow and temperature and computers adjust them accordingly. This is extremely important, given the one-to-one person-to-terminal ratio expected in the near future.

FIGURE 7–10 Infracon Lighting System

Easily installed in the suspended ceiling of an office, Infracon® automatically turns lights on when people enter the office and off when they leave.

Photo courtesy of United Technologies Building Systems Company.

Additional savings are provided by an automated security arrangement. The need for security guards decreases when doors and elevators are equipped with their own security devices, such as coded card keys. These are easily reprogrammed when tenants change and reduce the time required to secure changes.

Savings also result from using a fire management system. Should a fire break out, it is detected through a combination of smoke detectors, heat sensors, and occupant-activated fire alarms. The location of the fire is reported to the EMCS central processing unit, which sounds alarms to evacuate occupants. In addition, fire-fighting personnel are automatically notified, while stairways and other critical passageways are pressurized with outdoor air to prevent them from filling up with smoke. Thus, the fire is contained and response time is minimized. The result can be a great savings in life and property.

Labor and maintenance costs can also be reduced when all automated building systems are contained in one EMCS. By such consolidation and control, the productivity of the labor force increases. Failures and excessive wear of plant equipment can be reduced through automated maintenance scheduling.

The above functions should be integrated into an EMCS when fire management involves a significant amount of air handling in smoke control (fans, dampers, pressures, safety device overrides, etc.) or requires security system involvement (unlock doors). The ventilation systems of intelligent buildings are designed to pressurize floors above and below a fire to prevent it from spreading. This requires significant air handling and the ability to automatically lock and unlock doors.

The greatest benefit of a comprehensive, integrated EMCS is that a building engineer can locate any problem in one building on a computer display (see Figure 7–11). Its effect on other systems can be analyzed, and the problem can be quickly and efficiently corrected. Once again, the bottom line is savings in time and money.

THE INTELLIGENT COMMAND AND CONTROL CENTER

An intelligent command and control center is a central location from which the performance of each branch and node in an information network can be monitored. A network cannot function effectively without this centralized control, especially if there are functionally separate systems.

FIGURE 7-11

At CityPlace, in Hartford, Connecticut, building supervisors have at their finger-
tips information that tells them such things as where the elevators are, which
floors are empty, and where the ventilating systems is switched on.

The functions of an intelligent command and control center
include the monitoring and managing of:

- Life support and comfort.
  Personal comfort environment.
- Wire management.
  Local area network (LAN).

Power system.
Computer system.
Telephone system.
• On-line power management.
Uninterrupted power supply.
Power generation.
Energy management.
• On-line building control.
Remote administration.
Simulations.
• Maintenance.
Repair and diagnostics.
• Traffic.
Flow.
Accounting and control.

Monitoring Function

A centralized monitoring system efficiently handles network control, offering distinct advantages over the usual decentralized systems. These advantages include economies in the administrative tasks associated with control-center development and maintenance. They also include improved productivity of control-center personnel because there is a concentration of expertise.

This command center provides operators with the means to monitor the performance of network components and the ability to test them and diagnose their defects. Monitoring can be performed by control center operators as it is needed or automatically on a periodic basis. The automatic monitoring of components should inform the operators of any deterioration in the performance of a component before it actually malfunctions and causes a problem.

Diagnostic Function

Operators should have display terminals readily available through which they can gain access to and view the functioning of the systems in the network. From those terminals, they can investigate the status of software and hardware and directly perform a variety of diagnostic and repair functions.

Whenever possible, network control also provides the means whereby the operators can solve problems involving defective components. The components to be diagnosed include the transmission channels of the LAN, the switch, processors (such as mainframes and microcomputers) and terminating equipment (terminals and other devices that are sources or destinations of information transmission).

Whatever the transmission mediums or the equipment involved, it is necessary to identify network problems and take steps toward remedying deteriorating or failing performance. For a control center to be effective, operators must determine the effect that the failure of one component will have on other network components.

How an Intelligent Command and Control Center Operates

The intelligence of the control center is directly related to the degree to which its functions are automated. In order to provide the highest quality service to users and reduce problem-related costs, data and voice communications links are examined periodically by computer-driven devices. These devices perform a series of tests and record the results. When a test result lies outside prescribed limits, a message appears on the printer in the control center and is also logged against the offending component in a large, computerized database. This database allows the operators to keep track of the history of each of the systems and their components.

It is desirable, however, to automate the process further. Even if test results are not outside acceptable limits, symptoms may appear that would indicate to an expert investigator the probability of a particular defect appearing within a determinable time. This function is in the realm of simulations, artificial intelligence, and expert systems.

A greater degree of automation is also possible. At major nodes in the network, software-controlled matrix switches can be installed. When the system finds, for example, that a private line shows potential for trouble, the line is switched out of the network when it lies idle. A standby line is then switched in as a replacement. The control center operators then receive a description of the problem and the line identifier from the computer. A repair function is then followed. Using this process, no user would ever see a problem with the line under investigation. It would be taken out of service before a problem developed, serviced without any interruption or degradation of service, and returned to use in a trouble-free condition.

Effective Command and Control Centers Mean Cost Savings

The effectiveness of the control center is directly related to the degree to which its functions are automated. Effectiveness can be measured in terms of costs saved in strict dollars and cents.

Implementation of a fully developed, highly automated control center is a major undertaking. It is expensive and requires meticulous planning. The rewards, however, are commensurate with the effort. They include:

- Better control of the information network facilities and components.
- Higher quality service to tenants.
- Centralized liaison with vendors and carriers.
- Economies of scale.
- Centralized reporting capabilities.

An economic analysis of the typical problem an organization incurs will show—at least on a qualitative basis—why such a center is a worthwhile investment for any organization that maintains its own information network.

Each organization must determine the costs it will incur during each phase of a problem and the various impacts of one component on another. The life of a problem is marked by five events:

- The occurrence of the problem.
- The detection of the problem.
- The isolation of the problem to one particular subsystem or piece of equipment.
- The correction of the problem.
- The return of the system to normal operation.

During each phase of the problem, costs are incurred. It can be argued that costs mount the most rapidly during the first two phases. In order to reduce the total incurred cost, efforts can be concentrated on the second and third events, reducing the time from problem occurrence through its detection to isolation. An intangible benefit of shortening these events is improved network service.

Detailed planning of organization requirements, including involvement of the system's end users, is considered the essential prerequisite to automating office activities. A necessary component of this planning process is a consideration of the building design implications of automation.
Arthur Rubin,
Center for Building Technology–National Bureau of Standards

The Impact of Information Technology on Buildings and People

INTRODUCTION

Four factors are currently influencing office building design. Separately, each one influences all building development. Together, they are a powerful catalyst for the emergence of intelligent buildings. These factors are:

- *Technology:* Information technology mechanizes office work. It is likely to change every aspect of office life and the size, shape, servicing, and location of office buildings.
- *Society:* Workers are demanding control over every aspect of working life from opening windows, enjoying daylight and view, to maintaining acoustic privacy.
- *Energy conservation:* Concerns over rising energy costs are changing not only the outer shell of office buildings but also their systems.
- *Increasing professionalism of facilities managers:* Facilities managers are expressing their needs for buildings that will adapt as needed to dynamic organizational requirements.[1]

Evolving information technology is the most obvious of the changes in intelligent buildings. Less obvious is the role that technology plays in the other factors. Technology makes possible building automation, which allows for energy conservation through efficient building management. Technology can also negatively affect the work environment, leading to social change as knowledge workers—professionals and managers who use information technology in everyday work applications—voice their objections to the deteriorating quality of automated office environments. Technology therefore requires better planned facilities to meet human needs in modern offices, which is the job of facilities managers.

The reaction to unproductive work environments is summarized by the title of a draft from the Center for Building Technology, "The Automated Office: An Environment for Productive Work, or an Information Factory?"[2] "Information sweatshops" can be prevented only if the impact information technology has on buildings and people is assessed, and methods are devised to counteract them. This chapter examines this impact and some solutions.

NEGATIVE IMPACT OF INFORMATION TECHNOLOGY ON BUILDINGS

The impact of information technology on the office building environment can negate the benefits of building and office automation. These effects must be identified and steps taken to compensate for them. Information technology affects the office environment through creating:

- Temperature changes.
- Increased noise vibration.
- Static and dust.

Temperature Fluctuations

All electrical and electronic equipment generates heat. The automated office has more electronic devices and systems than the traditional one. Hence, the amount of heat they produce can substantially increase the building's cooling load. This can lead to equipment outages and occupant discomfort. Although few pieces of equipment give off more heat than a human being, a ratio of one person to each terminal effectively doubles the cooling load most buildings are originally designed for.

In addition, the heat emitted by equipment tends to be highly local and unpredictable, depending on the devices that are running at any one time. Furthermore, air conditioning systems with poor zoning contribute to uneven temperatures over large floor areas, and attempts to cool machine rooms may result in entire floors being cooled. The above factors point to a need for an energy management and control system (EMCS) that has an air conditioning system with zoning controls and monitoring.

Noise Vibration

Most electronic equipment generates noise. Like heat, noise is cumulative. A subtle problem is that distraction caused by noise is not directly related to volume. Its frequency, rhythm, and tone all contribute to noise pollution. Therefore, while such electronic devices as computer terminals are quieter than mechanical equipment such as typewriters, their noise can be more irritating to the human ear.

Acoustic hoods can help in less noisy situations, but they pose access problems for operators. Impact printers are the only significant source of vibration, but they may be mounted on shock absorbent mats that also serve to reduce noise. Certain pieces of equipment must be insulated in special rooms.

The advent of voice-activated systems will increase the office noise problem. These systems rely on spoken commands for instruction. An increase in office partitioning can provide one solution to the noise generated by voice-activated systems and to noise problems in general.

Static and Dust

Electrostatic discharge can be a major problem in an automated office. Static electricity is created in two ways:

- *Induction charging:* Electrical fields radiate from the surfaces of materials such as Styrofoam and cloth. For example, a shirt sleeve can generate enough of an electrostatic charge to destroy the read-only memory (ROM) of a computer memory.
- *Contact charging:* In contact charging, two materials make contact and then separate, causing one material to strip

electrons from the other. This occurs when one walks across a carpet and is shocked when touching a doorknob. The danger to information equipment is that voltages as low as 3,000 are sometimes sufficient to disturb computer circuits.

Common sources of static electricity are:

• Waxed, painted, or varnished surfaces.
• Vinyl tile flooring.
• Polystyrene (Styrofoam).
• Finished wood or plastic covered desks and chairs.
• Electrostatic copiers.
• Insufficient humidity.[3]

Management can take various safeguards, such as placing grounding between each electronic device and the main system-earth connection, avoiding synthetic carpets, using antistatic mats adjacent to equipment, and using earthed carpets. A more novel method of reducing static is installing ionisers, or negative ion generators. Most offices containing banks of electronic equipment are depleted of negative ions not only because the equipment tends to become positively charged, but also because air-conditioning ducts are positively charged. This neutralizes negative ions that occur naturally in air.

Dirt in the air—dust, pollution, and cigarette smoke—encourage and attract static as well as damage equipment. An unclean atmosphere reduces hardware life, particulalry that of removable hard disks, and causes prematurely high error rates in all magnetic storage media. This sensitivity means that a pressurized air filter is essential wherever central processing equipment is extensively used.

Printers, particularly high speed impact types that put paper through rapidly also product dust. The problem of dust coming into contact with magnetic storage media has to be solved by segregating printers and other dust-producing devices.

NEGATIVE IMPACT OF INFORMATION TECHNOLOGY ON PEOPLE

More than 5 million personal computers (PCs) are used commercially, and the PC population is steadily growing (see Figure 8–1). By the early 1990s, some 60 percent of business employees will use at least one personal computer, according to Future Comput-

FIGURE 8-1 Growth in Personal Computers

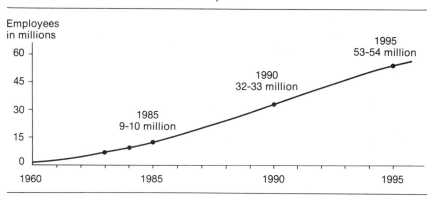

ing, a Dallas market research organization.[4] But personal computers are only one type of information technology used by knowledge workers in automated offices. Dumb terminals, word processors, and CAD/CAM systems are other keyboard devices becoming popular. The consulting firm of Arthur Andersen predicts a one-to-one ratio of workers per keyboard device by 1990 (see Figure 8-2).[5]

The influx of electronic devices into the office is too often seen as a goal rather than a means to an end. Understanding the difference is critical. The reason for automting should always be

FIGURE 8-2 Workers Per Keyboard Device

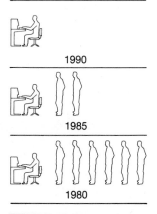

to increase office efficiency and productivity and thereby increase profitability. But automation alone will not necessarily maximize productivity or profitability. The people factor in the office picture must also be taken into account. The key element of managing that factor is planning to integrate the new electronics with the other systems already in place in the office and in the building itself. "Technology is the engine that drives change in the modern office," says Don Korell, director of research for Steelcase, Inc.[6]

New devices and systems are routinely introduced into offices designed to accommodate traditional paper-based activities. Many of these systems are noisy (e.g., printers, optical character recognition devices), and produce heat which must be properly dissipated. These can be uncomfortable for workers, and inadequate consideration of these and other impacts leads to a deterioration of the quality of the office environment. This has prompted the statement that, "The darker side of automation is the potential decline in workers' health and well-being."[7]

Evidence is growing that office automation equipment poses potential health hazards to workers. This is reflected in surveys of office workers that cite the inappropriateness of traditional surroundings and furnishings for monitor-based work.[8] According to a research summary published by the Bureau of National Affairs, Inc., using monitors can lead to body strain, and vision and stress problems.[9] In addition, job satisfaction among workers in automated offices tends to be low.

The culprit is the personal and other computers, their monitors, and related peripherals (i.e., printers). The problem emerged as technology and communications combined to provide the individual with immense information processing power and networking capabilities. The costs of this power to users are:

- Increased workstation space requirements.
- Specialized lighting needs.
- Noise of printers interfering with future voice entry devices, and the need of nearby workers for a quiet work environment.

Space

An example of the impact information technology has on space requirements is word processors. "Word processing workstations sometimes really do demand 75 percent more space than electric typewriter workstations," according to office design specialist, Walter B. Kleeman, Jr.[10] The number of devices that an office worker uses is increasing, making it necessary to also increase the size of the workspace. In addition, the conventional keyboard will be supplemented by touch pads, activated surfaces and, eventually, voice-entry devices. Each will make different demands on the workstation.

The increased work surface and storage space, in turn, steadily increases the number of square feet required by each electronic office worker. The picture becomes more complicated as the demand for private offices also increases. There is an apparent worker antagonism directed to open office planning and design. However, "Continued innovation in computer and elec-

FIGURE 8–3

Minimize office space but maximize individual space. This is the challenge to office planners today. Compact 10' × 10' workstations from Steelcase Inc. offer primary and secondary worksurfaces and an Ultronic 9000 adjustable VDT stand with a pull-out keyboard shelf. The total configuration promotes comfort and productivity.

SOURCE: Exploration and Production Systems Group, Tenneco Oil Company, Houston, Texas.

Photo courtesy Steelcase Inc.

tronic capacities will significantly reduce the size of terminals, printers, and other hardware. In addition, a decrease in requirements for paper viewing space will come about," according to Lawrence Lerner, chairman of Environetics International Inc., one of the nation's largest office design and space planning firms.[11] Thus, until miniaturization reduces space demand, managers need to plan on more space per worker (see Figure 8–3).

Changed Lighting Needs

Lighting is an example of an evolving need (see Figure 8–4). Lighting in traditional buildings is high intensity, uniform ceiling lighting with centralized switching. This type of arrangement creates problems for people using new technologies. For example, it causes reflections on display screens and does not allow for

FIGURE 8–4 Types of Illumination

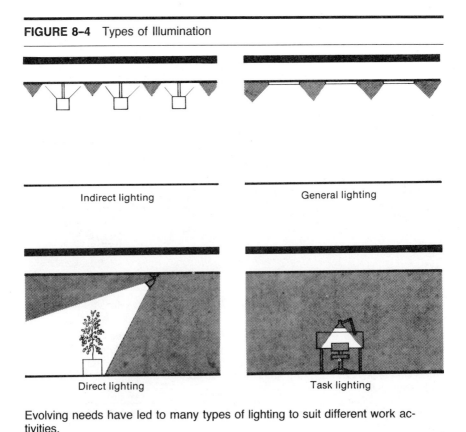

Indirect lighting

General lighting

Direct lighting

Task lighting

Evolving needs have led to many types of lighting to suit different work activities.

individual modification of lighting levels. Lack of modification can lead to eye and back strain among computer users.

Paperwork requires high levels of light compared to work at a monitor, although both kinds of work are frequently done at the same time. In addition, errant light from windows and artificial lights cause screen glare, reducing visibility of monitor-based work. Screen glare is the particular problem area noted in most surveys.

Lighting is, therefore, a main source of concern from office workers performing monitor-based activities. A major challenge for lighting designers is accommodating activities that require monitor, paper, and microfiche reading in the course of a single task. Some recommendations are:

- Lighting levels should be appropriate for activities performed. The quality and quantity of lighting should support the visual needs of those performing monitor and/or paper-based tasks.
- Individual control of task and area lighting should be available.
- Lighting should not produce glare.
- Extreme brightness and contrast should be avoided.
- Daylight should be appropriately integrated into the overall lighting system.

A number of recommendations have been made to reduce glare:

- Drapes, shades, and/or blinds over windows should be adjusted or closed, especially where there is direct sunlight.
- Terminals should be properly positioned with respect to windows and overhead lighting so that large bright areas will not be reflected on monitors.
- Direct-lighting fixtures may need to be recessed and baffles used to prevent the fixture from creating a glare.
- Walls and other surfaces should not reflect lighting.
- Desks and other work surfaces should have matte finishes and medium-tone colors; black or white surfaces should be avoided.
- Screen filters should be considered as methods of reducing glare on monitors.[12]

Many new buildings include ambient lighting (see Figure 8-5). These are general lighting schemes which wash over work areas

FIGURE 8-5 Ambient and Task Lighting

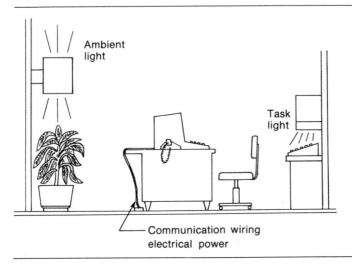

without creating glare. They are often supplemented by task-oriented lighting directed by the user (see Figure 8-4). These lighting systems are both ergonomic and economical, as they often cost 40 percent to 75 percent less than those commonly used in older buildings.[13]

Acoustics

Surveys of office workers have identified noise as a major problem area in the automated office.[14] Presently, printers are the primary noise source. Auditory and visual privacy are also prominently mentioned by workers, especially those occupying open-space offices. Among the suggestions made to offset some acoustical problems are:

- Separation of noisy equipment from the general work floor.
- Surface treatment of space with sound absorbing materials such as fiberglass insulation and cloth-covered panels.
- Placement of acoustical barriers to reduce noise transmission from one space to adjoining areas.
- Designing offices to avoid sound transmission paths between spaces, protect auditory privacy, and minimize noise intrusion.

- Use vibration-damping techniques to prevent material from resonating to a primary source, e.g., place an acoustical barrier between a printer and a tabletop.[15]

In the near future, voice-entry systems may demand substantially higher levels of acoustic isolation in the workstation.

Paper

Until video storage and system networking come of age, the computer will continue to be the greatest paper generator yet devised. Its hard-copy printers generate reams of reports (see Figure 8–6). Don Korell, of Steelcase, claims that, "In the United States alone, computers churn out enough paper each day to

FIGURE 8–6 "The Life and Hard Times of the Paperless Office"

circle the earth 40 times, about double the output of copy machines."[16] One reason for such paper production is that workers and jobs simply require more information at one time than the half-page screen displays.

The impact of technology on people must be compensated for before the work environment can fully support its workers. In addition, recent studies indicate that an important component of job satisfaction is the ability to personalize one's work area and have some degree of control over it.

THE ROLE OF FURNITURE

The growing importance of office furniture in productivity is underscored in a recent study by the American Productivity Center in Houston. The study reports that

> today's factory worker is backed by a $25,000 average investment in equipment, compared to a $2,500 investment for the office worker . . . [However] as white-collar productivity becomes increasingly important, capital investment in the office will quadruple, reaching $8,000 to $10,000 per worker by 1989. Most of the money will be spent on electronic equipment and task-supportive office furniture.[17]

Furniture, lighting, communications distribution, and acoustics used to be separate areas of interest. Now, furniture manufacturers are looking beyond the worker's traditional needs of desk and storage space, to pieces designed to cope with the proliferation of computers (see Figure 8–7). Meanwhile, industrial design focuses on combining areas previously in the domain of interior designers and architects.

The two key ingredients of furniture today are:

- *Flexibility:* the ability to adapt to evolving office needs.
- *Adjustment:* the ability to "tune" the overall office environment to each worker's special ergonomic needs.

Flexibility. Furniture systems must adapt to the individual's needs. In the automated office, the individual's immediate work environment is the workstation and its furnishings. Two things are happening to change office workspace requirements. First, the number of electronic devices each worker uses is increasing. Second, paper is increasingly being replaced by electronic and microfiche-based systems. The individual's workstation must ac-

FIGURE 8-7

Scientific studies continue to stress the importance of the overall environment in increasing office productivity. *Where* people work—how that space looks, how it is organized—definitely affects *how* people work. At Steelcase, a continuing effort is being made to determine the best and most effective ways too apply systems furniture to the "electronic" office. New and innovative planning principles are being developed at the company's new corporate headquarters. These are illustrated in its showroom above, as well as throughout the 385,000 sq. ft. administration building located in Grand Rapids, Michigan.

Photo courtesy Steelcase Inc.

commodate workers processing information on all these devices in all of these forms at a single workstation.

Technological advances are being made so rapidly that there is an overriding need for design flexibility to accommodate changes as they occur. Flexibility often means the ability of workstation components to be easily changeable, since very responsive office workers "do change the configuration of workstations as many as 10 times per year if the work demands it,"[18] according to Walter B. Kleeman, interior office design expert (see Figure 8-8).

Flexible furniture designs also help people cope with the problem of wire management (wires on top of, inside, and under

---

FIGURE 8-8 Workstation Flexibility Is a Must

Trend: increasing organization flux
Impact: frequent workstation
relocation and functional change
Need: Flexible, 100% modular
furniture and service delivery systems

---

today's computer-topped desks). As part of the furniture, these designs take the form of boxes, pipes, and "overgrown rubber bands." In addition to considering wiring, furniture manufacturers are providing lighting systems as part of their furniture designs. These can be task and/or ambient lighting, depending on the design.

Furniture systems now also include paneling. The open office is still very popular, and many of today's open office areas are panel-hung. These are work surfaces and shelves that are supported by dividers below ceiling height. However, freestanding equipment, which is more modular than funiture systems which include paneling, is growing in popularity for two important reasons: it is more flexible than panel-hung designs and allows for much greater emphasis on ergonomic design. Furniture manufacturers are investing in companies that manufacture relocatable floor-to-ceiling walls, an indication of the direction that furniture manufacturers are taking.

Adjustment. A recent study of the National Academy of Science cited the design of the workstation and job features as critical to monitor-based work.[19] (See Figure 8-9). It points to the need for accommodating differences among individual workers with respect to their physical attributes and preferences. Among the findings in this investigation and others are the following:

- The individual should have some say in the design and selection of his or her furnishings and equipment and an opportunity to personalize the workspace.

FIGURE 8–9

Working at a VDT screen for long hours can often cause eye fatigue. To counter this problem at the Milliken Customer Center in Spartanburg, South Carolina, wall hangings in bright, vivid colors are used to create a sense of space and also provide a visual diversion from the VDT screen. Operators can look up over panels and focus on distant walls. In addition, tan workstation panels provide low-contrast backgrounds for VDT screens. This Milliken solution utilizes the total office environment to deal with one problem created by new technology.

Photo courtesy Steelcase Inc.

- Special, separate devices are recommended so workers can adjust the height of work surfaces, key board levels, source documents, and terminal screens.
- Chairs with high backrests and adjustable inclinations are recommended.
- Forearm/hand supports should be available for keyboard work, and keyboards should be movable.[20]

Furniture designers, working to meet the need for flexible and adjustable furniture, are:

- Producing adjustable desks and chairs for people of different heights and sizes (see Figure 8–10).

FIGURE 8-10 The Humanetics® Fully Adjustable Workstation

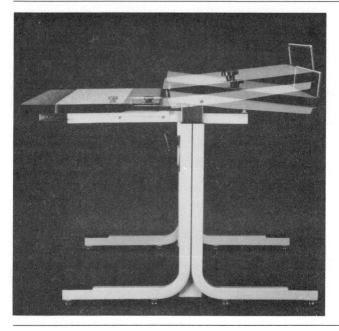

Photo courtesy of Tab Products Company.

- Emphasizing high touch with an endless selection of fabrics, shapes, colors, and textures (see Figure 8–11).
- Making furniture modular, so that only one or two pieces will become obsolete as requirements change.
- Testing to guarantee everything is ergonomically designed for the user's comfort.
- Installing casters on, or otherwise making furnishings readily portable for today's changing office environment.

Paying more than lip service to work-area design does go straight to the bottom line.

INFORMATION TECHNOLOGY AND NEW ORGANIZATIONAL SPACE NEEDS

The impact of information technology, methods of coping with it, and changing work patterns affect tenant space planning. For instance, "Organizations or sections whose day-to-day work methods were previously unaffected by computers could in one year

FIGURE 8-11 High Touch Furniture—An Antidote to Today's High Tech
Equipment

Ten or 15 yers ago, two desks in a corner might have been considered sufficient, but today it's recognized that office professionals need new tools to be
effective in increasingly sophisticated and demanding jobs.

Photo courtesy Steelcase Inc.

reach a stage where 80 percent of workplaces had a computer
terminal."[21] Such rapid change calls for flexible space planning.

A striking feature of information technology developments is
the radical and fast transformation it brings about in organizations. Most organizations' reaction to this transformation produces barely controlled chaos. So much equipment is introduced
so quickly, and changes happen so often, that planning the *details*
of the physical environment becomes an unattainable ideal. This
typically results in the constant rearranging of floor plans and
desk layouts.

Even if changes do not increase in frequency, they are becoming more difficult. Tenants will therefore value design features
which simplify space planning.

Space Planning

In the past, space planning was largely ignored by managers.
Many assumed that automation offered the answers to all produc-

tivity concerns. Those who purchased new furniture systems with modular pieces assumed they had a flexibility which could meet all advances in office systems or adapt to any necessary reorganization. Furniture, however, does not by itself answer all tenant space needs. Planning the office space—where the furniture goes and what people need in their own workspaces—is an increasingly important dimension of managing office automation. Not only individual workspaces are important. Conference rooms, high touch rest areas, libraries, rooms with specialized equipment to share, and quiet rooms for work that demands intense concentration must all be planned for. Space planning as a whole is becoming more professional as it evolves to meet the needs of organizations using information technology.

Managers are integrating physical layout, design, and communications to support organizational objectives that:

- Emphasize informal information or conversational exchange.
- Call for periodic changes in work teams and study groups.
- Provide employees with access to specialized equipment.
- Value individual initiative and mobility.
- Attract talented employees.
- Increase productivity while reducing office costs.

What Does This Mean for Space Allocation?

Organizational space allocation is likely to change. Up to 50 percent of floorspace will be set aside for meetings, conferences, training, relaxation, machine rooms, and so forth. Further allocations will depend on a company's preference for open-plan office design or private offices. A company committed to open offices with partial partitions can consider whether people have sufficiently quiet surroundings to perform tasks that require concentration. Open-plan offices may therefore require a greater number of private work areas used on a shared or reserved basis.

Overall, the tenant may need more office space than in the past. Some specialists, however, challenge this view as shortsighted. Between 1985 and 1995, Philip J. Stone and Robert Luchetti expect that "there will be less paper storage, computer terminals will become smaller or embedded into desk surfaces, home bases consequently will become smaller, and shared setting for specialized equipment will proliferate."[22] In this case, the increased need of rooms for specialized equipment and uses may still mean greater space requirements on the part of tenants. Once again, flexibility in space planning is called for.

Coherent rethinking of an office plan requires that management integrate facilities, communications, and computers in accord with company objectives.

Developers need to ask the question: What kind of office space ought we to be providing?
Dr. Francis Duffy
Architecture and Space
Planner

Intelligent Building Features: A Response to Information Technology Requirements

INTRODUCTION

Information technology affects building design both directly and indirectly. Directly, the added machines mean increased wiring, heat generation, and space requirements. This calls for more ducts, more cooling, and more generous space standards. Information technology affects building design indirectly by changing organizational structure. For example, it causes a decline in the numbers of clerical workers, introduces more complex forms of decision making, and allows flexibility of working hours and locations. The impact these organizational changes may have on office buildings are at least as important as the direct effects of information technology.

INTELLIGENT BUILDING DESIGN

The direct and indirect effects of information technology point to the following five major areas of consideration in building design:

- Flexibility in overall building design.
- Space requirements.

- Air conditioning.
- Special machine rooms.
- Wiring.

Flexibility

The introduction of office automation equipment requires more than providing adequate wiring. Most intelligent buildings house a number of tenants who are in different occupations. These are tenants who cannot economically justify the purchase of their own information equipment and choose shared tenant services (STS). Intelligent buildings must be designed flexibly enough to accommodate these smaller tenants and the equipment or services they need. Less uniformity throughout an office building is therefore needed.

A recent research project sponsored by Xerox Corporation took an in-depth look at the office of the future.[1] The study was conducted to determine what would be needed, and which options would be available in updating existing structures to accommodate new technology. A major conclusion of "Office '88" was that there is a need for built-in flexibility in structures. Flexibility must encompass the actual base building, such as the floor configuration and ceiling heights; available systems, such as heating, ventilating, cooling, electrical wiring, and telecommunications cabling; and components such as walls, lights, ceilings, carpeting, and furniture. The bottom line of intelligently designed buildings is *flexibility*.

Space Requirements

The greatest impact on space is the individual workstation and its peripherals, such as printers. "As the individual workstation gains acceptance and is provided with increasing capabilities (and devices), it requires more space than the system which it replaced," according to Arthur Rubin.[2] In general, the space requirements of information technology are underestimated for three reasons:

- Devices are bulky, especially when keyboards are integral to the unit. Besides terminals, a number of items are required for enquiry and data entry tasks, such as reference books, microfiche viewers, dictaphones, desk-top disk storage, and printers.

- Extra space is needed for such ancillary and support functions as enclosures for printers, areas for disk storage, rest areas, and meeting and training rooms. The ratio of ancillary space to desk space is obviously increasing. In some offices, only half of the net usable space is occupied by workplaces.[3]
- Paper must be stored effectively until other storage methods become widely available and are accepted.

The old space-planning rules of thumb—based on space required per person—need to be drastically revised as a result of these trends. Many businesses are finding themselves unexpectedly growing out of their premises because they underestimated the amount of space required solely for equipment.

Air-Conditioning

It is critical to have an air-conditioning system capable of meeting a variety of cooling requirements in the intelligent building. Impact on building design arises from both people and machines being in the same office area, increasing the building's ventilation and air-conditioning requirements. It has been suggested that the heat load of a computer terminal is about the same as adding another person to the work area. Workstations can have high heat output, perhaps 40 watts per square meter. If all workers have a computer, the effect is the same as doubling the staff size, as previously mentioned. Most buildings have simply not been designed to handle this sort of burden. One solution is localized environmental cooling/conditioning that is relocatable and can be programmed by the individual.

In addition to heat created by personal workstations, concentrations of equipment require more of air conditioning systems. Most equipment tolerates a wider range of thermal conditions than human beings. However, concentrations of central processing equipment generally require some extra cooling for two reasons: (1) the heat output from equipment is considerable and can easily rise above levels suitable for equipment as well as for people and (2) temperatures for machinery, of whatever level, should be kept even, with changes of no more than 1 degree F per hour, in order to avoid shrinkage and expansion of tapes and disks, etc. (See Chapter 3, Life-Support Systems, for a more complete discussion on air conditioning.)

In addition, many devices are humidity sensitive. Humidity control is essential for the proper operation of equipment and for minimizing the detrimental effects of static electricity. Ideal humidity conditions are around 50 percent (at 70 degrees F). If relative humidity is too high, moisture absorption and dimensional changes may occur, causing paper handling devices to jam. If humidity is too low, static is produced.

Special Machine Rooms

The introduction of personal computers or microcomputers is not likely to reduce requirements for specially segregated and environmentally controlled machine rooms. More offices will need machine rooms for housing large, powerful computers or peripheral equipment such as printers, to provide control of temperature, humidity, dust, noise, and static electricity. However, the number of machine rooms available in intelligent buildings is likely to increase. These rooms will be dispersed throughout the building rather than concentrated in one area. Machine room requirements can vary between:

- *Minimal:* a partitioned space having some degree of sound proofing, antistatic carpeting, extra cooling, and window coverage to reduce solar glare, as well as the prohibition of smoking or beverages in the room.
- *Maximal:* a sealed space with a raised floor for extra wiring needs, intensive 24-hour air-conditioning, special fire precautions, shuttered windows to prevent solar glare, secure access, a standby generator, and, in some cases, an uninterrupted power supply.

The accommodation of computers and disk drives in these special rooms:

- Protects staff from heat output.
- Reduces maintenance problems.
- Provides a stable environment for equipment that needs even temperatures at all times, not just during office hours.
- Simplifies monitoring and supervision.

Wiring

An intelligent building should contain enough room for the cabling/wiring required by the building information systems and their peripherals, while providing the means for easy and convenient movement and removal if necessary. Wiring systems must meet the following four criteria:

- *Capacity:* The ability of a cable system to feed entire electronic and communication systems.
- *Flexibility:* Speed and low cost of adding new outlets or taking out old outlets.
- *Life-cycle cost:* Economy and performance of a cabling system, from construction throughout a building's life cycle.
- *Aesthetics:* The concealment of wires to maintain the uncluttered appearance so prized in modern integrated office environments.

Office automation requires an immense amount of wiring. What may be miles of cable must be threaded through the building walls and floors, and cabling connections need to be highly concentrated and flexible for shifting workstations and equipment. "Wiring . . . was cited by several design firms as being the most important planning consideration and the most difficult and expensive one to accommodate. Equipment types, densities, and locations are all subject to future changes, so these systems must be designed to move and be adaptable," according to Arthur Rubin of the Center for Building Technology.[4]

Problems in wiring or cabling include:

- Choking of ducts with old, unwanted cables. It can be costly and difficult to remove these cables.
- Insufficient number of ducts and outlet points, making it difficult to access wires and wire new areas.
- Lack of capacity to hold additional cable ducting. Ducting is the traditional method of wiring a building. Insufficient room in ducts is the reason old buildings must often be retrofitted before intelligent building technologies can be incorporated.
- Trailing cables at the workplace and coils of surplus cables hanging behind desks. These are mild safety hazards, but they impede workstation flexibility and ruin office aesthetics (see Figure 9–1).

The responsibility for wiring a building, once provided by the telephone company as part of its complete telephone service installation, has now passed to the building owner. Owners have a choice of providing wiring themselves or hiring a third party to do

FIGURE 9–1 Trailing Cables from Workstations

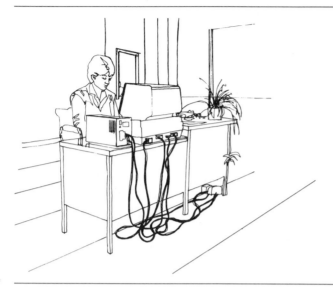

so. Wiring can be owned and/or managed by a party other than the building owner, such as the system provider. However, it is recommended that building owners and managers own and manage the wiring in their own buildings. Ownership is critical in issues of access and system control, particularly if a dispute over moving wires or removing old wires arises. In this sense, building wiring accommodations and equipment should be treated as any other building feature. And, in buildings utilizing control features such as energy mangement, system and wiring ownership encompasses control of all tenant offerings in the building.

Building wiring design must accommodate present and future needs. While internal building facilities are being engineered, extra capacity for data and voice transmission requirements should be planned. This provides total connectivity within buildings and eliminates the future need to rewire or pull new wires for additional data device requirements.

Typical wiring systems include:

- Ceiling systems.
- Raised floors.
- Underfloor ducting.
- Electrical cellular deck.

- Floor drilling or "poke-through."
- Flat wire.

Ceiling systems.   Many buildings provide ceiling systems for lighting and other types of wiring. An important component in ceiling distribution systems is full height walls through which cabling can be brought from the ceiling to well-placed outlets. Open-plan offices sharply reduce the amount of full-height walls available for cabling, however. The use of ceiling wiring for heavy cabling needs remains a significant problem in modern open-plan offices. This is leading to the growth in popularity of floor systems, although their capacity is more limited than that of ceiling systems found in older buildings.

Raised floors.   Raised floors were first used in special computer rooms for housing bulky cable harnesses, return-air ducting for air-conditioning, and fail-safe power circuits. When computer terminals moved into the office, raised floors were not considered necessary for their use. Raised floors used in computer rooms were not designed or priced for general offices, nor easily retrofitted into existing buildings. Two trends influenced the growing use of raised floors in the office:

- More workstations were being outfitted with terminals.
- The practice of rearranging workstations developed.

As the numbers of office devices grew, the need for increased and flexible wiring caused builders and architects to consider solutions offered by raised floors (see Figure 9–2). Raised-floor manufacturers contributed to this momentum by designing sys-

---

FIGURE 9–2   Raised Floors

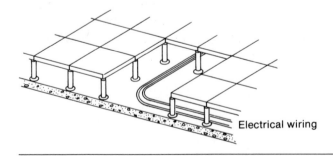

Electrical wiring

tems specifically for general offices that provided more afford-able life-cycle-cost analyses.

Easier wire management is not the only reason raised floors are gaining popularity. The trend toward smaller, decentralized building automation systems creates the opportunity to incorporate HVAC (heating venting air conditioning) systems into the floor and gain additional benefits (see Figure 9–3). *Task air,* or air that such systems deliver directly to workstations, can be controlled individually by users to create "micro climates."

Furthermore, when mechanical systems are combined in a floor with wiring, the initial expense of the raised floor can be amortized over a broader base. However, the flexibility of a raised floor provides dividends that accrue each time a workstation is moved or a new terminal added. This is important, because the initial cost of a raised floor is often higher than that of other wiring distribution systems.

Raised floors are offered in many configurations to suit different applications and budgets. Heights vary from 4 to 30 inches, depending on the number and type of services to be housed. They are generally installed 4 to 7 inches over the structural slab for electrical wiring applications (for telecommunications and office automation) and at heights of up to 30 inches for adding mechanical building automation systems (such as HVAC or air conditioning ductwork). The 30-inch floor void can also be used to accommodate distribution wiring for power, telephone, and computer networks in an efficient and increasingly cost-effective manner.

FIGURE 9–3 Raised Floors Accommodate Other Services

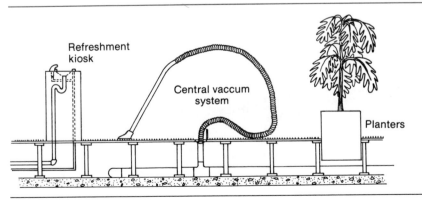

A raised-floor system consists of panels, normally 24- by 24-inches, and adjustable pedestal assemblies. Carpet tiles preserve access to the floor void. To eliminate carpet waste, some manufacturers offer pre-upholstered panels with carpet cut exactly to panel size.

Expected developments include lower installation costs, improved acoustics, and new varieties of long-wearing coverings. More flexible wiring and greater use of the floor void for housing other building systems such as lighting, plumbing, security, and telecommunications are also expected.

Since other wiring systems often serve the same purpose at a lower cost, raised floors are not always the answer. However, given the increasing demand for flexibility and the greater complexity of services, their use is on the rise.

Floor drilling or poke-through. In this system the floor slab is cored so that electrical wiring can be pulled up from the floor below (see Figure 9–4). The resulting holes must be fire-treated. The conduit runs from its connection to the service fittings of the slab to the space junction box. A sleeve may be preset during construction or after. Once the hole is drilled, a sleeve is forced into place, and the service fittings are installed from above.

Floor drilling, or poke-through, provides access to wires when they are needed in new locations or when retrofitting older buildings that lack vertical and ceiling space. However, it is a solution of last resort since it offers little flexibility and, if done in excess, weakens floor structures. It is, in addition, often against local fire codes.

FIGURE 9–4 Poke-Through System

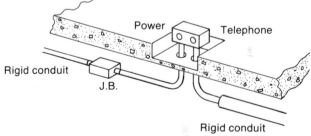

FIGURE 9-5 Underfloor Ducting

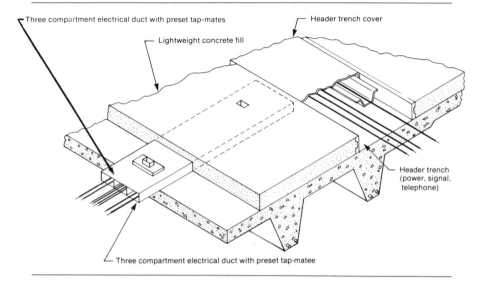

Three compartment electrical duct with preset tap-mates

Lightweight concrete fill

Header trench cover

Header trench (power, signal, telephone)

Three compartment electrical duct with preset tap-matee

Underfloor duct. Buildings have traditionally been wired through the conduits or duct space under the floors (see Figure 9-5). This is a much cheaper alternative to installing a raised floor. However, the underfloor duct system has a limited volume capacity and access holes which may not be ideally located. This limits the flexibility of most duct systems, which are therefore unable to meet expanding wiring needs. Flexibility is the key word in designing intelligent buildings, and the wiring system is the key component.

Electrical cellular deck. This system consists of closely spaced cellular "raceways" (or area ways) under the floor that connect at regular intervals to a main and header duct (see Figure 9-6). A matrix of preset service fittings is spaced just below the surface floor in a raceway. Cabling is accessed by punching a hole through a thin raceway panel and bringing the appropriate cables through the opening and up through the floor.

Duct and cellular floor systems, with their neat, gridlike approach, allow an outlet to be placed within about two feet of any point required. These systems allow low-cost wiring distribution

FIGURE 9-6 Cellular Deck

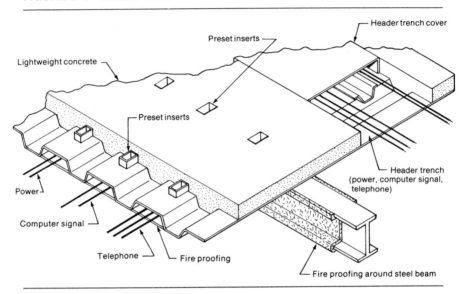

modifications to be easily made. However, the built-in redundancy of the grid system and the duct work itself mean that initial costs of floor cabling systems tend to be high.

Flat wire.   Flat wire, shaped to fit between a slab and carpet, provides an alternative to ceiling or floor cabling. It has rapidly become a popular system for branch wiring applications because of its special capabilities and the advantages it offers for use in both old and new buildings.

A flat-wire system is composed of the following main components:

- *Transition boxes:* connect conventional building wiring with flat cables.
- *Tap and splice assemblies:* permit cables to branch off main runs or be added to existing ones.
- *Outlets:* permit services delivered via flat wire to be accessed and utilized wherever desired.

These building blocks, a layout to determine their placement, and the carpet tiles that cover them comprise a complete system. The special capabilities of flat wire are:

- Ability to interface with virtually any distribution system and unobtrusively deliver services to any point on a slab.
- Ability to move outlets, or add others later, without disrupting occupants and at a cost that is competitive with that of other systems. It requires no special work during construction, or core drilling later on, and can be used to add new "reach" to existing wire management systems. It is also handy for retrofitting buildings requiring additional capacity.

TABLE 9-1 Tradeoffs among Alternative Wiring Systems

System	Positive	Negative
Poke-through	Low first cost No raceway	Expensive to make changes Disruptive of activities Fire precautions needed
Electrical cellular deck	Relatively flexible Easy to make changes	Expensive Servide fittings sometimes protrude; unsightly, tripping hazard
Underfloor duct	Accessible No fire safety problem	Expensive Difficulty designing for needed flexibility
Raised access floor	Integration of electrical communications, HVAC Flexible	Expensive to install Disruptive, hazardous when frequent changes made. Many spaces need conventional floors—ramps, stairs needed
Ceiling-based systems	Easy to integrate with furniture systems through walls Flexible	High first cost Careful planning needed—intrusive
Flat cable	Short installation time Structural integrity of floor system kept Changes can be made readily Can be used under carpets	Cable must be shielded from punctures Careful installation needed to avoid unsightly cable ridges

SOURCE: NBSIR 84-2908, Interim Design Guidelines for Automated Offices, August, 1984, p. 66. Center for Building Technology/National Engineering Laboratory/National Bureau of Standards/Gaithersburg, Maryland 20899 and Public Buildings Service/General Services Administration/Washington, DC 20405.

Flat wire is also attractive because of the potential savings allowed by taking investment tax credits or accelerated depreciation, since the cable is not a permanent part of the building. It is also unnecessary to advance capital to install outlets or duct work before space is rented or occupied. This is extremely important in a multitenant intelligent building.

As in applying many new technologies, architects and engineers have held back from implementing flat wire in view of its possible shortcomings. These include possibly higher costs than anticipated, less capacity than hoped for, the need to use insulated carpet tiles, and the visibility of the wire through the carpet. In addition, heavy, sharp objects dropped on a cable can penetrate a conductor, or coffee spilled onto live cables can present a potentially major problem. In either case, a surge of current might flow back to the panel box through the cable or its ground top shield and trip a circuit breaker.

Despite the drawbacks of a flat-wire system, architects and engineers increasingly specify flat wire for both new and repeat applications. Manufacturers are refining their designs for added flexibility and developing new parts so that their systems will be compatible with rapidly evolving telecommunications technology. (See Table 9–1 for comparison of wiring systems.)

DO EXISTING OFFICE BUILDINGS MEET INFORMATION TECHNOLOGY REQUIREMENTS?

Have existing office buildings been designed to incorporate information technology? Do they have the air conditioning systems, the flexibility, or the wiring capacity? The ORBIT Study[5] concerns a number of buildings in the United Kingdom and their capacity to integrate information technology. An important part of the ORBIT study sampled a range of 22 existing buildings in the United Kingdom and their ability to cope with information technology. Coauthor Michelle D. Gouin interviewed architect Rigomar Thurmen regarding the applicability of the United Kingdom study to the American office-buildings market.[6] Prof. Thurmen discussed the existence of building design standards which have caused post–World War II buildings to be similar in design, whether they are in Omaha or Singapore. Given these standards, it is safe to review the results of the ORBIT Study in a worldwide context, as only one of the 22 buildings sampled is of the prewar

TABLE 9–2   Interview with Professor Rigomar Thurmen

Q: What are the possible differences in design between office buildings in the United Kingdom and the United States?

A: The standard of office design . . . the state of the art is equal . . . to what I have seen of recent buildings in England. The same technology is used on a worldwide basis, since the same firms are doing work in Omaha and Singapore.

Q: What time frame are you alluding to when you say 'recent'?

A: Whatever has been published anywhere from six months up to two years ago.

Q: Would you say, then, that buildings 10 to 20 years old will differ substantially from country to country?"

A: The state-of-the-art even since 1965 . . . the technology and design principals have been quite international for office buildings. This is true for the era following WWII . . . after recovering from the effect of WWII. They might have some minor differences, but the general concept is the same. Air-conditioning has uniform requirements, regardless of outside temperatures (seal buildings off), which set international standards. I don't think there is much difference today between any of the Western Nations: Singapore, United Kingdom, Italy, Germany, America.

era (see Table 9–2). In order to assess buildings, their characteristics were matched against the following:

- What is their capacity? Which kind of high-tech changes can be easily accommodated in the building as it exists now? For example, are more vertical and horizontal cabling, more cellularization, or additional cooling possible?
- How adaptable are they? How easily can the tenant effect changes as technology develops?
- How easy are they to retrofit? How easily can the builder carry out major changes in the building?
- How manageable are they? How much effort and cost has to be put into running the building on a daily basis?

The ORBIT Study subsequently converted each of these four main user criteria of performance into a number of separate measurements. For example, one measure of capacity is the percentage of usable area of a given office floor which can be converted into single office rooms, each of which enjoys an outside view. Another is the ease with which services such as wiring are accessed if modifications have to be made.

Using these measures and with the aid of plans and sections drawn to the same scale for each of the buildings in the survey, a panel of study team members and outside consultants assessed the sample buildings. The team rated each of the 22 buildings covered by each measure using a simple five-point scale—5 representing excellent, 4 good, 3 fair, 2 poor, and 1 very poor (see Table 9–3). ORBIT Study results showed that the buildings in the sample varied widely in their performances. Rarely did they score well or badly in all categories. For example, a building which had a great deal of capacity to accommodate, route, or adapt cabling had far less capacity to handle zoning.

Results of the ability of the typical London office building to support the influx of automated devices showed that about 80 percent of the offices were incapable of providing either adequate lighting, cabling, heating, ventilation, or air conditioning. In some cases, floors were strong enough to withstand the weight of information devices.

The study therefore indicates that the majority of available office-building space is typically highly inflexible and unable to provide high-density office automation. Carpeting is often high-grade broadloom, which is not easily recut and repatched.Ceiling and corresponding light grids are permanent and inflexible.

TABLE 9–3 Orbit Study Sample Results

		Capacity	Adaptibility	Buildability	Manageability	Average Score
Spec built	1	3.2	2.3	3.5	3.0	3.00
	2	3.2	2.3	2.5	3.0	2.75
	3	3.2	1.8	2.5	3.3	2.70
	4	3.7	2.5	3.5	3.0	3.18
	5	2.8	2.3	3.0	3.7	2.95
	6	2.0	2.3	1.0	3.0	2.08
Deep open plan	7	2.8	2.5	3.5	3.0	2.95
	8	2.3	1.8	3.0	3.0	2.52
	9	2.7	2.5	3.5	1.3	2.50
	10	3.0	2.5	3.0	2.7	2.80
	11	3.2	3.0	3.0	3.3	3.13
	12	2.2	2.8	2.5	2.7	2.55
Industrial	13	2.3	3.5	4.0	4.0	3.45
	14	2.5	2.8	3.0	4.0	3.08
General	15	3.0	2.3	5.0	3.7	3.50
	16	4.5	4.8	3.5	3.0	3.95
	17	2.8	2.8	3.5	3.0	3.03
	18	3.7	2.5	3.5	4.0	3.43
	19	3.7	3.3	4.0	2.7	3.43
Tower	20	2.2	2.3	2.5	3.0	2.50
	21	3.2	2.0	2.5	2.7	2.60
	22	3.7	3.0	3.0	3.3	3.25

HVAC systems are designed around the traditional heat loads and diversity factors. Electrical power capabilities are below that demanded by today's high-performance electrical workstations. The increase in office automation has placed additional strain on the utilities in existing office buildings. "Many buildings will lose tenants simply because the utility system cannot meet the demands," according to Michael Clevenger, the principal consultant of office standards for Xerox Corporation.[7] "Some buildings were designed with only a few HVAC zones on each floor to contain building costs. With the move toward automation, it will become important for developers to have many small zones to deal with the extra sources of heat," Clevenger added.

An examination of the offices in the United States suggests that as we approach one terminal for every five and fewer workers, a notable percentage of current facilities are overloaded in at least one area.

COSTS OF ADAPTING TO NEW REQUIREMENTS

The cost of adapting buildings to accommodate information technology or renovating them can be very substantial, according to the ORBIT Study.[8] In many cases, the cost of renovating a building approaches the cost of building a replacement. Furthermore, the massive work required is disruptive and causes huge productivity losses during the renovation period. When a building has historical value, however, the costs of renovation may be negligible compared to the building's value to the community and its tenants' need of information services. Extensive and premature renovation of some buildings will therefore be expensive but inevitable. For others, renovation may not be cost-effective. Some buildings may become prematurely obsolete, since their design does not allow flexible planning or servicing provisions.

For architects, ORBIT suggests, "The challenge is first to set standards for new office buildings, and second to work out which existing office buildings are worth renovating. Knowledge of what information technology means and willingness to help all potential tenants understand its implications should mean not only new kinds of building but new kinds of service."[9]

Intelligent Building Business Plan

Management and Corporate Goals

- Strategic:
  Evaluate new products and technologies.
  Develop cost-competitive services.
- Risk management:
  Industry trends.
  Technology scan.
  Government regulations—impact of PUC rulings.
  Tenant composition.
  Developer/tenant trends.
- Critical path:
  Qualitative and quantitative goals.
  Targets.
  Time frames.
  Expected results.
- Administrative management:
  Procedures/methods needed.
  Timing and approach.
  Quantify benefits to developer/owner.
    Enhances building image.
    Attracts new tenants to building.
    Improves and protects property values.
    Improves building and facility management.
    Remains competitive.
    New technologies.
- Organizational structure:
  Management team—strengths/weaknesses.
  Construction projects—develop interfaces.
  Organizational structure.

- Project management:
    Programs and projects.
    Prioritization.
    Timing and scheduling.

Products and Services

- Evaluation and selection.
- Development cycles—estimation.
- Segments, product substitutes, size and growth, seasonal or cyclical market, share of market, rate of technological change and system obsolescence.
- Integration—existing equipment with newly acquired equipment.
- Sales/marketing.
- Product literature.
    Quantify tenant benefits:
    Cash flow.
    Overall cost savings.
    Convenience—one-stop shopping for equipment, local services, long-distance, maintenance, and administration.
    Centralized management—need to deal with one management.
    Responsiveness—ability to expand or contract services quickly support.
    Reliability—higher than in-house system.
    Availability of capabilities and features not otherwise affordable due to size.
    Training—available as needed.
    Professional management.
- Promotion, advertisements, sales cycle (prospect to installation).
    Selective presentations to:
    Large tenant—facility manager.
    Small tenant—principal/owner.
- Pricing, credit policies, leasing and rental options.
- Field engineering support activities.
- Training support:
    Initial training.
    Ongoing training.

Financial and Legal

- Five-year projections of profit and loss with supporting assumptions.
- Staffing levels, compensation, and organizational chart.
- Capital projections, services projections, facilities projections, personnel requirements (hiring, maintenance, training development).
- Capitalization, credit lines, leasing agreements.
- Contingent liabilities, pending litigation.

Audio Bridge Features

- Twenty-four port teleconference capacity.
- Microprocessor controlled with automatic answer and instructions by voice synthesizer.
- Access by off-premises DTMF (dual tone multifrequency) tone dial key pad.
- Software allowing subdivision of teleconference into simultaneous sub-teleconferences.
- Automatic-gain amplification compensating for network losses, to provide high quality audio to each participant.
- Security features via touch pad which lock out undesired participants.
- Software customized to user's operational requirements.
- Monitor jacks that provide operator interface, if desired.
- Individual status lights on each port module that allow for talker identification.
- Expander jack which allows linking of two systems for full 48-port configuration.
- Twenty-four hours a day access from any telephone in the world network.
- Compatibility with all types of amplified speakerphones or teleconference systems.

Integrated Voice/Data Features

An integrated telephone and computer system should provide the following:

- Fully featured circuit switching for voice and data at appropriate speeds.
- A switch with a bandwidth of up to several hundred megabits to accommodate thousands of voice and data terminals.
- Contention-switched access over twisted-pair telephone wiring.
- Fully featured data processing system.
- Office-system software, including word and text processing, electronic mail, file storage and retrieval, calendar and scheduling tools, personal computing, and conferencing capabilities.
- Gateways to local networks.
- X.25 interfaces—CCITT standards to provide compatibility of data processing equipment.
- Access to IBM hosts—to make use of large amounts of hardware and software developed by IBM.
- Physical and functional integration.
- Wide area network access.

Such system integration will offer virtually all of the capabilities required in a modern office environment. The multitenant intelligent building contains the wiring and information equipment which support these capabilities. This allows for interconnection of the telephone network, word and text processing, electronic mail, file storage and retrieval, calendar and scheduling tools, facsimile, personal computing, and conferencing capabilties.

PBX Generations

Confusion over generation designation of PBXs may be a problem. This is not helped by the controversy in the industry itself over what constitutes a fourth-generation PBX. A brief description of the generations will not only clear up this point but also illustrate why at least a thrid-generation PBX is necessary in an intelligent building.

First-generation PBXs, now considered obsolete, include electromechanical, crossbar, and electronic crosspoint systems. Manually driven, their switching capabilities are extremely limited. Second-generation PBXs were the first so-called intelligent PBXs. Because they are software driven, they overcome the limitations of manually driven PBXs. Automation allowed for the economies of multiple use of transmission mediums, through both frequency division and time division multiplexing. However, due to the analog form of transmission, only voice communication is easily supported by second-generation switches. The nature of data communications demands digital switching.

The need for digital switching explains the necessity of third-generation PBXs in an integrated voice/data scenario. Integration of voice and data means the PBX is designed to handle both voice and data on an equal basis without separate transmission paths, sub-multiplexing schemes, alternate use ports, dedicated voice and data ports, or doubling up of ports required when both voice and data are handled. Third-generation PBXs support simultaneous data and voice transmission with data rates up to 65 Kbps.

At this point, there is much controversy surrounding third- versus fourth-generation PBXs. Some solve this problem by listing the characteristics under a general third/fourth generation title, arguing that the improvement of fourth generation PBXs lies in their increased transmission speeds and the inclusion of a local area network (LAN) into their architecture. Others state that

175

this distinction does not warrant the designation of a new generation title. According to W. Spencer Rice, senior partner of S&R consultants:

> The difference between second and third generation architectures represented a quantum leap in switch design. . . . The difference between third and fourth generation is nothing less than a quantum leap in technology.

Using this criterion, Rice establishes the following characteristics of both third and fourth generation PBXs.

Third-generation PBXs:

- Have a digital switching matrix, using PCM coding.
- Have a non-blocking architecture, i.e., for each station installed there is at least one time slot not otherwise spoken for by registers/senders, control signals, and so forth.
- Incorporate multiple main or shared processors of 16- or 32-bit type to handle real-time call processing, input/output functions, port scanning, and so forth.
- Use very large scale integration (VLSI) in processors, memory, and port cards to reduce size, power requirements, and heat output.
- Are voice digitized at the handset rather than at the port card or system level.
- Have some speed, format, and protocol conversion at the circuit-card level, rather than at system level or through stand-alone converters/minicomputers.
- Use a high-level computer language to program the system generic software and applications software (allows the user to customize or create his or her own software using generally available programming skills).
- Have a tightly coupled local area network (LAN) for workplace and building data communications at high bandwidths.

Fourth-generation PBXs:

- Use optical switching technologies (Mbps rates).
- Use a fiber-optic backplane with multiple buses (Gbps).
- Have fully integrated office automation subsystems.
- Have distributed/shared processors and software (firmware).
- Have megabit memory densities (optical).

- Make extensive use of firmware and on-chip ram/prom.
- Have extensive error correction and redundancy.

Fourth-generation PBXs, on a marketable scale, are still 15 years in the future. However, the third-generation PBXs now available have sufficient capabilities to switch the equipment contained in an intelligent building.

Software for Intelligent Buildings

PBX Management Software

An attraction intelligent buildings have for developers is their ability to turn the costly old telephone system center into a sophisticated telecommunications profit center. Intelligent buildings offer more than a PBX; they offer shared tenant services. Managers of intelligent buildings need PBX software which does more than SMDR to assign costs.* Shared tenant services can be a large profit center, and managers want sophisticated traffic management and invoicing capabilities to reap these profits (see Table 2-1).

PBX management software enables a building manager to do two things: manage the network's capacity and allocate telephone costs accurately and appropriately. It provides the tools for managing telecommunications costs and network performance. Reports are designed to:

- Identify abuse.
- Allocate costs to extensions and departments.
- Measure trunk use and identify trunk groups with extremely high or low usage.
- Bill back to client account codes.
- Rate calls accurately according to appropriate tariffs.
- Identify WATS overflow in ARS systems.
- Recommend optimal system configurations.

Managers and tenants have different requirements. Property managers of office complexes need to offer their clients greater capabilities at lower cost. This means shared tenant services (STS) and sophisticated invoicing. Their concerns include:

---

* See Appendix D for Station Message Detail Record (SMDR) data.

- Are all trunks carrying traffic properly?
- Is the quality acceptable?
- Which trunks are down?
- Is there the right number of trunks in the network?

Tenants need to track expenses reliably in order to allocate costs, which demands advanced report generation.

The most effective way to satisfy these varied demands is called *attached processing*. In essence, it means attaching a computer to the PBX or CENTREX to make telecommunications "work smarter," and produce higher profits. It takes more than automation to turn telephone costs into profits. Management is still an important consideration. Management systems monitor traffic, and statistically derive running averages of level, noise, and return loss for each circuit. They also compute average call duration, total traffic, data traffic, and report dropout or level deviation of modem carrier on dedicated data circuits. Exception reports and management reports can both be provided.

Exception reports. The first step is to specify the acceptable limits for parameters of the telecommunications network. When these have been keyed into the PBX management system, an exception report with data and time tag is issued when a parameter on a circuit strays outside these limits. Date and time of correction of the deviation are also reported.

Exception reports allow the network to be managed as tightly as chosen, without the need to wade through reams of reports in order to find bad circuits. Exception reports find:

- *Low and high levels.* Low levels on only a few trunks can cause complaints that appear to be the fault of the whole trunk group. High levels can cause echo or distortion of touch-tone digits, resulting in frequent misdials.
- *High noise.* Finding noisy circuits is sometimes difficult as the noise level varies over the course of the day. A management system which records the beginning and end of each high-noise period eases detection of noisy circuits.

    Average noise level also varies among common carriers, and these systems can help route calls through carriers with the least troublesome circuits.
- *Low return loss.* Poor return loss on certain circuit terminations can cause echo problems on satellite or other circuits.
- *Modem carrier dropout.* This provides immediate notification of carrier dropout through an alarm.

- *Short average call duration.* Short calls can indicate a faulty switch port or a malfunctioning trunk.
- *Hung trunks.* Excessive off-hook time can mean a trunk is carrying no traffic.
- *Idle trunks.* If one trunk is idle too long while the rest are carrying traffic, it may be an indication of excessive trunks or a dead trunk.

Such functions allow managers to spot problems on voice and data network before they affect services. Managers can actually be called by the system when a circuit does not meet the set performance limits, thereby saving time.

Management reports. These provide information on all monitored circuits, giving a broader view of the telecommunications network. Reports include:

- *Traffic management reporting.* Provides telecommunications managers with information that helps ensure more efficient use of the network. The information for use in traffic analysis reports is derived from SMDR data, providing a complete analysis of current trunk facilities based on traffic patterns. From these, optimal configurations for calling patterns can be derived.
- *Traffic summary.* Provides information on traffic per hour on each trunk, reported for a 24-hour day. This report allows maintenance of the optimum amount of traffic on each trunk group and allows spotting problems in hunt sequence.
- *Network configuration.* Analyzes present configuration during average busy hour for total use, grade of service, average queuing time, overflow, total cost, and cost per minute.
- *Call distribution.* Computes by hour for each type of service in present configuration and gives total use in hours, erlangs, grade of service, and percent of total usage for a given time period.
- *Data traffic summary.* Provides information on data traffic per hour on each trunk, reported for a 24-hour day. Shows how much data traffic, if any, is overflowing from data networks and if data is a sizable portion of total traffic at any time during the day.
- *Call duration.* Provides information on the average length of calls, reported separately for incoming and outgoing calls. This data finds killer trunks or bad switch ports by showing

unusually short average call durations. It also finds hung trunks by showing unusually long call duration. Exception reports are issued for any circuit exceeding set limits.

- *Transmission parameters.* Provides the current average value of level, noise, and return loss, the three parameters most affecting transmission quality. With this report, overall quality of common carriers can be compared.
- *Bad call percentage.* Shows the percentage of calls on each circuit that have fallen outside set limits for level, noise, and return loss.
- *Tariff files.* Contains complete and up-to-date tariff files for local message units, DDD, WATS, MCI, and SBS services.

Such reports may also:

- Compute recommended configuration for average busy hour.
- Indicate break-even points for additional trunks based on hours of usage and costs.
- Present recommended configuration for each trunk or trunk group in terms of:
    Total usage.
    Grade of service.
    Total number of calls queued.
    Average queue time.
    Overflow.
    Total cost.
    Average cost per minute.

The management report presents current and proposed configurations. For the current configuration, the report lists existing trunk facilities, the number of lines in each trunk group, usage per trunk group, total cost per trunk group, and average cost per minute per trunk group. With this report, unusual conditions can be easily identified (e.g. trunk groups with very high or low usage and/or costs).

The second part of the management report presents the recommended configuration for the most cost-effective combination of trunk groups to efficiently handle offered traffic. This recommendation is based on the following: whether the system is queued or nonqueued; measured busy-hour and active-hour information; working days in the month and business hours in the day; the current grade of service; and the required grade of service. The recommended configuration specifies where to add and remove lines from a trunk group and where to add new facilities. The average time in queue per trunk group is computed for queued systems.

An additional report may identify traffic overflowing from the first choice to other types of facilities and calculates the cost of the overflow. For trunk groups with higher than acceptable overflow, the optimal number of lines for the trunk group can be determined. This report also identifies incorrect routing patterns and compares the overflow costs of alternate routes to the cost for the primary route.

Call cost accounting. The capability to price telephone calls includes different rate structures to allow call costing of specialized common carriers (SCCs) and special trunk groups.

Invoicing. Provides the ability to bill for telecommunication usage, as well as both telecommunication and non-telecommunication equipment, services, and one-time costs. This customizable invoicing is especially valuable in the shared tenant services environment.

Such a tenant resale billing system issues:

- Summary and detailed use reports.
- Accounts receivable reports.
- Revenue reports.

Financial reports. Summarizing the invoice information, numerous financial and management reports are produced to track revenues and receivables, maintain customer records, and provide audit trails. These reports include:

- Customer master file listing—Contains pertinent history information for each tenant.
- Accounts receivable in customer name sequence—Lists tenants in alphabetical sequence by tenant name. Included is the status for the customer's account as well as the date and amount of the last payment.
- Accounts receivable in customer number sequence.
- Interim payment report—Provides a complete audit trail of all payments applied to each tenant's account. It shows the date of the payment, the batch number of when payment was entered, the application code (payment applied to 30, 60, or 90 day balance), the payment amount, and the remaining balance due.

- Payment proof listing—Provides an audit trail to reconcile applied payments to actual bank deposits. Each deposit is identified by a batch number.
- Adjustment audit—Provides an audit trail of all adjustments to each customer's account. The report shows whether the adjustment is a debit or credit, the balance to which it was applied, the amount, the date, and the batch number to identify when the adjustment was entered.
- Adjustment summary—Provides a summary of the total number and dollar amount of adjustments applied during the month by adjustment code category.
- Monthly and year-to-date summary revenue reports—Provides a composite summary of all the revenues and adjustments for the current month.

Telecommunications costs are getting to be among the largest uncontrolled business expense today. Increased use of the telephone for telemarketing, sales support, or customer service is commonplace. Today, use of the phone by virtually every employee of a company is an accepted part of many businesses. In the future, the phone system will be used to support electronic mailing and teleconferencing.

Telecommunications costs can be monitored and efficiently controlled to capture the benefits derived through the increased use of the phone system. The above systems illustrate some of the functions of PBX management systems, designed to maximize use of the telecommunications system.

SHARED TENANT TELECOMMUNICATIONS SOFTWARE

The following is a list of software features suggested for an intelligent building management information system (MIS):

Tenant Order Processing

- Tenant management:
  Occupant file maintenance.
  Occupant transaction processing.
  Escalation billings.
  Retail sales processing.
  Residential tenant reports.
  Commercial tenant reports.
  Management fees.

Lease analysis.
Archiving.
- Tenant processing:
  Transaction posting.
  Late charges.
  Security interest credits.
  Invoices.
- Commercial/residential reports:
  Tenant directory.
  Building profile.
  Recurring charge list.
  Open item aging.
  Tenant receivable statements.
  Commercial expiration report.
  Cash receipts journal.
  Billing and collection summary.
  Rental income in square feet.
  Tenant history reports.
- Disbursement processing:
  Vendor file maintenance.
  Process vendor invoices.
  Process manual checks.
  Write checks from vendor invoices.
  Check reconciliation.
  Recurring bills processing.
  Vendor invoice allocations.
  Owner's distribution.
  End of month.
  Vendor inquiry.
  Archiving.
- Payroll processing:
  Employee master directory.
  Time sheets.
  Payroll report writer.
  Check register.
  Quarterly reports.
  Print W2 forms.
  Employee file maintenance.
- Financial statement processing:
  Operating statement by property.
  Income statement by property.
  Balance sheet by property.

Operating statement by tenant.
Income statement by tenant.
Balance sheet by tenant.

Telephone Order Processing

- Maintenance:
    Service orders.
    Customers.
    Vendors.
    General ledger control.
- Service order processing:
    Customer.
    Vendor.
    Status.
    Part number.
- Reports and procedures:
    Print service order.
    Print job order.
    Service order report generator.
    Customer reports.
    Archiving.
    Vendor comparison.

Inventory

- Maintenance:
    Master file.
    Vendors.
    General ledger control.
    Facility file.
- Transactions:
    Receipts and adjustments.
    Repairs list maintenance.
- Inquiries:
    Installed equipment by part number.
    Installed equipment by cable pair/route/port.
    Intalled by customer.
- Reports:
    Report generator.
    Audit trail tracking.
    Archiving.

Place month markers in audit trail.
Vendor list.

System Control and Reporting

- Maintenance:
    System definition.
    Message rates.
    Call rates.
    Tax files.
    System stations control.
- Inquiries:
    System call history by cost center.
    Graphic traffic analysis.
- Reports and procedures:
    Call rates report.
    Call detail report errors report.
    Hourly activity report.
    Summary of frequently called numbers.
    Call distribution report.
    Summary of calls by date.
    Summary of calls by area code.
    Trunk traffic report.
    Unbillable call detail report.

Billing and Accounts Receivable

- Maintenance:
    Customers.
    Departments.
    General ledger control.
- Transactions:
    Customer adjustments.
    Receive payments.
    Call history.
    Transfers/deletions.
    Account receivable by customer.
    Billing cycle status.
- Reports and procedures:
    Customer directory.
    Aged trial balance.
    Year-to-date sales and collections.

Month-to-date sales and collections.
Batch summary report.
Customer listings.
Invoice register.
Closing cycles.
Demand invoices.
Archiving.
Register maintenance and report.

General Ledger Interface

- Maintenance:
  Account.
  Current transaction.
- Inquiries:
  Accounts.
- Reports and procedures:
  Account listing.
  Current transaction.
  Posting current transaction.
  Archiving.

Trouble Reporting

- Maintenance:
  Log or update trouble.
  Log or update corrective action.
  Maintain trouble codes.
  Maintain corrective action codes.
- Reports and procedures:
  Traffic summary.
  Data traffic summary.
  Holding times.
  Transmission parameters.
  Bad call reports.
  Exception reports:
    Holding times.
    Idle time.
    Levels.
    Noise.
    Return loss.
  Trouble report generator.
  Archiving.

- Inquiries:
    By equipment type.
    By number.
    By status.
    By trouble date.
    By trouble code.
    By user.
    Call detail report.
- Transactions:
    Equipment database update.
    Facilities database update.

Directory Assistance and Publication

- Maintenance:
    User setup.
    Master file.
    Publishing format.
- Inquiries:
    On-line directory information.
    Directory search.
- Transactions:
    Change directory.
    Status board.
- Reports:
    Sorted by name.
    Sorted by organization.
    Sorted by cost center.
    Sorted by title.
    Sorted by extension.
    Print directory file.
    Archiving.
- Customer service:
    Reports troubles.
    Changes basic data.
    Examines customer account.
    Invoices adjustments.
    Removes users.
    Adds new users.
    Changes users.
    Deactivates account.
    Calls history inquiry.
    Releases pending notification.

Traffic Analysis

- Maintenance:
  Peg counts.
  Usage.
  Delay.
- Transactions:
  Study periods.
- Reports:
  Facility recommendations.
  Problem identifications.

Station Message Detail Recording (SMDR)

Within seconds of receiving a completed call record from the PBX, the cost for that call is calculated and stored in the PBX software management system. Each call is priced by actual cost, direct-dial assessed cost (to indicate savings realized by specialized services), and penalty cost (if least-cost route was not used). In addition, any amount of percentage can be added to or subtracted from each phone call. A minimum charge can also be established per call. This enables assessment of equipment charges as well as actual phone cost to the user.

Network costs if services are to be added or changed can also be analyzed. For example, the effect of adding WATS Band 3 service to the system could be calculated.

Reports available within SMDR subsystem include:

- Call detail by extension:
    Listing of calls and charges for each user.
    Summary of incoming calls.
- Call summary:
    By department, division, and corporation.
    Comparative analysis by percentage.
- Budget analysis, detail, and summary:
    Department, division, and corporate summaries.
    Equipment cost analysis.
    Comparative analysis by percentage.
    Period-to-date and year-to-date analyses.
- Extension ranking (cost or time):
    Highest to lowest cost or usage.
    Exception reporting.
- Call ranking (cost or time):
    Longest or greatest individual cost.
    Exception reporting.

- Calls by account (project code):
  Billing by project and/or authorization code.
- Cost by route:
  Cost comparisons of each area code dialed on a particular route.
- Area code summary:
  Totals for each area code dialed.
  Optimal WATS service determined.
- Penalty costs by extension:
  Detects improper route usage.
  "What if" savings projections.
- Route advance cost analysis:
  Penalties incurred by PBX routing features.
  When to add a trunk.
- Off-hour call exception:
  Abuse detection.
- Called number ranking:
  Most frequently dialed numbers.
  Exception reporting.
- Call number watchdog:
  Dial-a-joke, OTB, sports, weather, etc.
  Best customers.
- Call detail inquiry:
  On-line, selective review of calls.
  Extensive exception reporting.
  Screen display or print.

CENTREX Features

Standard Features

- Add-on conference—incoming. Permits a CENTREX user to add another CENTREX station line into an existing conversation.
- Call transfer—incoming. Permits a station user to transfer any incoming call to another within the station.
- Consecutive station hunting. Allows the incoming call to ring to another station when the dialed number is busy, thus preventing lost calls.
- Consultation hold—incoming. Allows the user to hold an incoming call through switchhook operation and place a new call within the CENTREX for the purpose of consultation.
- Direct inward dialing. Allows incoming calls to be placed directly to the desired department or individual.
- Direct outward dialing. Allows station user to place calls without attendant.
- Identified outward tolls. Identifies originating station for every outward long-distance call.
- Interception of calls to unassigned number. Automatically intercepts calls placed to unassigned numbers within the CENTREX and directs the caller to a working number.
- Station-to-station calling or intercom. Allows any CENTREX station to call any other station by dialing four digits.
- Touch-tone dialing. Allows the use of touch-pad dialing.

Optional Features

- Alternate answering. Automatically transfers those outside callers who get a busy signal or no answer to another line for answering purposes.

- Automatic callback. Allows CENTREX user placing a call to a busy station to automatically be called back when both stations become idle.
- Call forwarding. Automatically reroutes an incoming call to any desired telephone, in or outside the CENTREX system.
- Call hold. Allows the user to hold any call by depressing the switchhook and dialing a hold code. The telephone set can then be used to place another call.
- Call pickup. Allows any CENTREX user to answer a call ringing at another station.
- Additional call pickup group. A feature which allows for additional pickup groups. For example, half of the lines may be in one group and the rest may be assigned to another.
- Call waiting. Alerts a station user on a call that another call is waiting. By using the switchhook, the user can hold the first call to answer the second. Using call waiting may also reduce the number of lines needed.
- Dialed conference. Enables the telephone station to establish a conference call involving up to six parties by dialing a conference calling access code.
- Distinctive ringing and call waiting tones. Allows the station user to determine the source of incoming calls by different ringing or tone patterns.
- Loudspeaker paging. Allows station users to dial a code for paging equipment access.
- Off-premises locations. Allows customers with multiple locations one-system convenience when CENTREX stations are installed at other business locations.
- Recorded telephone dictation. Permits access to, and control of, customer-owned telephone dictating equipment.
- Reminder ring. Provides a one-half second ring at stations with call forwarding.
- Speed calling. Enables user to place any call by dialing one or two digits.
- Speed dialing. Lets the user dial frequently called numbers with a simple code. It will allow a program of either 6 or 30 numbers for speed or convenience dialing.
- Three-way calling. Allows the station user to establish a conference call with parties in or outside CENTREX.

Stable and Competitive CENTREX Rates

CENTREX began to lose its luster in the late 70s. AT&T strategists believed that CENTREX could not compete against the new PBX offerings over the long run. As a state-regulated service, CENTREX lacked the price flexibility necessary to compete in a price-sensitive market. Under the Modified Final Judgment of 1982, the divestiture plan accepted by AT&T and the Justice Department, the Bell operating companies were prevented from providing enhanced and customer-premises equipment unless they set up separate unregulated subsidiaries.

Added to this picture is the FCC's access plan. Rather than allow long-distance users to continue to subsidize the local network through artificially established rates, the FCC determined that the AT&T breakup should serve as an impetus for a more rational rate structure.

The FCC proposed that the residential users should be charged a maximum of $2 a month per line beginning in 1984 and eventually pay a maximum of $6 a month per line in 1986. Business users would immediately pay a maximum of $6 a month per line. CENTREX users would pay a maximum of $2 a month per line for existing lines as of July 27, 1983. This monthly rate would increase $1 a year in 1985 and 1986. New CENTREX users' systems would pay the full $2 a month charge for their new CENTREX lines.

Under the FCC's modified formula, CENTREX users could still pay more than 10 times as much as PBX users in monthly fees. This is because each of the telephones in a CENTREX subscriber's office will be charged for tieing into the central office switch, while the PBX user will only pay for those trunks that carry external calls to and from the central office switch.

As a compromise, the Bell operating companies, state regulators, and CENTREX users proposed a PBX-equivalency formula to the FCC for determining the local access charges on

CENTREX subscribers. Under this proposal, a CENTREX user with 100 lines would pay the same overall charge as PBX users with trunking capability up to 100 lines. This proposal was based on the assertion that the bulk of the telephones and lines used by CENTREX subscribers are used for intraoffice communications. Therefore, their lines are not imposing an equal burden on the central office switch and should not be charged a flat rate. The proponents of this approach suggest that engineering data could be used to determine an appropriate formula. This issue has not yet been decided.

Possible CENTREX Features

Other possibilities for CENTREX include:

- Least-cost routing.
- Local in-WATS (800) intra-LATA* service.
- Feature rearrangements.
- Message center activity.
- Customized station telephones.
- Interface to energy management and other telemetry.
- Security systems.
- 9.6 kilobit data/switched modem pooling.
- Citywide and multicity CENTREX.
- Selective call forwarding.
- Distinctive ringing.
- Calling number display.
- Call rejection.
- Personal identification number services—such as automatic transfer machines (ATMs), which serve the banking public.

---

* LATA—Local Access Transport Area. These have been designated throughout the states by state commissions. A LATA may encompass more than one contiguous local exchange area. It is meant to serve common social, economic, or other purposes, even where area transcends municipal or other local governmental boundaries (see Figure 3–4).

Broadband Coaxial Cable Transmission

Broadband coaxial (coax) cable is currently the transmission medium for economical local distribution of high volume voice, video, and data. The broadband transmission capacity of cable is used to provide simultaneous transmission of many signals, in both directions, on a single cable. This technique employs a midband split, with essentially half of the capacity of the cable transmitting signals in the forward direction and half transmitting in the reverse direction.

Standard LAN Gateways

The trend has been for service users to develop gateways between each type of medium in use in an efficient and cost-effective manner. This allows for virtual connectivity, or the ability of a user to connect to any resource. One such gateway is the CCITT X.25 standard. The Consultative Committee for International Telephony and Telegraphy (CCITT), is an organization concerned with devising and proposing recommendations for international telecommunications standards. X.25 is a data communications interface protocol that permits data transfer to outside communications networks or packet-switching systems without further translation. Use of this standard permits access to outside data banks and more information. In this manner, both voice and data needs are met over a wide range of transmission speeds.

Intelligent Building Resource Guide

Professional Associations

The Urban Land Institute
1090 Vermont Avenue, N.W.
Washington, DC 20005

Multi-Tenant Telecommunications Association
For information, write:
Mr. John Daly
Telecommunications Manager
PRC Corporation
McLean, VA 22102

International Facility Managers Association
3970 Varsity Drive
Ann Arbor, MI 48104

Management Companies

Intelligent Buildings Corporation
Canyon Center, Suite 311
1881 9th Street
Boulder, CO 80302-5151

RealCom
8301 Greensboro Drive
McLean, VA 22102

Conferences and Seminars

Intelligent Buildings Conference
Cross Information Company
Canyon Center, Suite 311
1881 9th Street
Boulder, CO 80302-5151

Research Organizations

Cross Information Company
934 Pearl Suite C
Boulder, CO 80302

Legal Advisors

Pepper, Hamilton & Scheetz
1777 F Street, N.W.
Washington, DC 20006

Newsletters

Tenant
Phillips Publishing
7315 Wisconsin Avenue Suite 1200N
Bethesda, MD 20814

Energy Management Systems

Director of Marketing
Integrated Building Systems
HONEYWELL
Honeywell Plaza
Minneapolis, MN 55408

Standards Organizations

American National Standards Institute
(ANSI)
1430 Broadway
New York, NY 10018

American Society for Testing & Materials
(ASTM)
1916 Race Street
Philadelphia, PA 19103

Building Industry Consulting Service International (BICSI)
Center for Continuing Education
University of Florida
Tampa, FL 33620

C2 Committee (National Electrical Safety Code)
NESC Committee   IEEE
345 East 47th Street
New York, NY 10017

Computer & Business Equipment Manufacturers Association
(CBEMA)/X3 Committee
311 First Street, NW, #500
Washington, DC 20001

Electronic Industries Association (EIA)
2001 Eye Street, NW
Washington, DC 20006

Exchange Carriers Standards Association (ECSA)
4 Century Drive, 3rd Floor
Parsippany, NJ 07054

Institute of Electrical & Electronic Engineers (IEEE)
345 East 47th Street
New York, NY 10017

Institute for Interconnecting & Packaging Electronic Circuits (IPC)
3451 Church Street
Evanston, IL 60203

Insulated Cable Engineers Association (ICEA)
P.O. Box P
South Yarmouth, MA 02664

National Fire Protection Association (NFPA)
Batterymarch Park
Quincy, MA 02269

Protection Engineers' Group (PEG)
U.S. Telephone Association
1801 "K" Street, NW, #i201
Washington, DC 20006

Underwriters' Laboratories (UL)
1285 Walt Whitman Road
Melville, Long Island, NY 11747

U.S. Telephone Association (USTA)
1801 "K" Street, NW, #1201
Washington, DC 20006

Telephone Accounting Software

Account-A Call Corporation
4450 Lakeside Drive
Burbank, CA 91505

Communications Support Systems
123 Felton Street
Waltham, MA 02154

Conrac Corporation Alston Division
1724 South Mountain Avenue
Duarte, CA 91010

CP National
242 Old New Brunswick Road
Piscataway, NJ 08854

Honeywell Communications
Network Division
4401 Beltwood Parkway South
Dallas, TX 75234

National TelData Corporation
1556 North Woodland Drive
Saline, MI 48176

NEC Information Systems
5 Militia Drive
Lexington, MA 02173

Rolm Corporation
4900 Old Ironsides Drive
Santa Clara, CA 95050

Summa Four Inc.
2456 Brown Avenue
Manchester, NH 03103

Sure Communications Inc.
257 Park Avenue South
New York, NY 10010

Sykes Datatronics Inc.
159 East Main Street
Rochester, NY 14604

Teknekron Infoswitch
P.O. Box 29039
San Antonio, TX 78280

Tekno Industries
795 Eagle Drive
Bensenville, IL 60106

Teldata Systems
90 Broad Street
New York, NY 10004

Telecom Service Bureau
1134 Tower Lane
Bensenville, IL 60106

TMS Systems Inc.
180 Bear Hill Road
Waltham, MA 02154

Western Telematic Inc.
2435 South Anne Street
Santa Ana, CA 92704

Advanced Automation Concepts, Inc.
3760 Lower Roswell Road
Marietta, GA 30067

AMF Texas Controls, Inc.
P.O. Box 59469
Dallas, TX 75229

Centaurus Software, Inc.
4425 Cass Street, Suite A
San Diego, CA 92109

Industrial Computer Designs
31121 Via Collinas, Suite 1005
Westlake Village, CA 91362

System Software, Inc.
16302 Sealark
Houston, TX 77062

Tano Corporation
4301 Poche Court, West
New Orleans, LA 70129

VOCOM
215 North Cayuga Street, P.O. Box 847
Ithaca, NY 14850

American Consulting Engineers Council
1015 15th Street, NW
Suite 802
Washington, DC 20005

American Institute of Plant Engineers
3975 Erie Avenue
Cincinnati, OH 45208

Association of Energy Engineers
4025 Pleasantdale Road
Suite 340
Atlanta, GA 30340

Association of Professional Energy Managers
1 Market Plaza
Suite 3001
San Francisco, CA 94105

Building Owner's and Manager's Association International
1250 Eye Street, NW
Washington, DC 20005

The National Association of Energy Service Companies
2300 M. Street, NW
Washington, DC 20037

Energy User News
Fairchild Publications
7 East 12th Street
New York, NY 10003
(212) 741–4000

Energy Management Technology
Walker-Davis Publications, Inc.
2500 Office Center
Willow Grove, PA 19090

Glossary

ANSI—American National Standards Institute. An organization affiliated with International Standards Organization (ISO), which establishes standards for protocols, transmission codes, and languages.

ASCII—American National Standard Code for Information Interchange. A coded bit set of seven bit coded bits and a parity bit used for data communications, which defined 128 characters.

Access Charges. Business firms were assessed a $6.00 per line monthly access charge on April 3, 1984. CENTREX users were assessed a $2.00 per line charge. In June of 1985, residential telephone users will pay a $1.00 monthly access charge. These charges are intended to bring the price of local telephone service more in line with actual cost. Before divestiture, local service was kept well below actual cost through long-distance subsidies. With divestiture, long-distance subsidies are to be eliminated and replaced with marketplace pricing.

Address. A location within a computer operating system referred to in a software program. The location of a physically and/or electronically logical entity in a network.

Alphanumeric. All the characters of the alphabet and all special characters; also, numbers if treated as characters by a program.

American Telephone and Telegraph (AT&T). Since the divestiture AT&T is composed of AT&T-Communications, AT&T-Information Systems, and AT&T-Technologies. AT&T-C replaces Long Lines. AT&T-IS is the new name for American Bell. AT&T-IS is financially separate from the rest of the organization, as ordered by Computer Inquiry II. This marketing must be separate as it is unregulated, while the balance of AT&T is regulated. AT&T-T replaces Western Electric.

Analog. A communications channel or signal which uses a continuous electromagnetic waveform to convey information.

Analog Signal. A continuous signal that varies in direct proportion to the strength of an input signal. Telephones transmit the human voice by converting sound waves into electrical analog signals.

Artificial Intelligence (AI). Computer programming that recognizes ideas and answers problems. A system may have sensory perception. AI is used in robotics and "expert systems" where there is a base of specialized knowledge and a program from which a computer can solve problems.

Asynchronous. Not synchronized. Can be sent or received when participants choose, as opposed to fixed intervals.

Asynchronous Transmission. A method of transmitting individual ASCII characters that permits arbitrary spacing between characters.

Audio. The voice portion of a communications link.

Auto-Answer. A feature that allows equipment to automatically receive and store information or messages until the recipient requests them.

Audio Conferencing. Teleconferencing which allows individuals and groups to communicate through voice alone. Two-way voice communication between two or more groups or three or more individuals who are remote from one another and are using a telecommunications medium.

Bandwidth. The difference between the highest and lowest frequencies a transmission channel can carry. A standard telephone line generally can carry frequencies between 300 and 3,000 hertz (cycles per second), providing a bandwidth of 2,700 hertz. In terms of signal frequency, the range between the lowest and the highest frequencies used in a signal transmitted from one site to another. Bandwidth is a measure of an analog signal and is measured in cycles per second. Contemporary units are hertz (one cycle equals one hertz). The difference expressed in cycles per second between the highest and lowest frequencies of a band. Wider ranges (e.g. 6 million cycles per second, the bandwidth of a television channel) are called broadband. Frequency ranges of 3,200 cycles per second, or hertz, (the bandwidth of telephone voice transmission) is referred to as narrowband. The range of frequencies available for transmission of data over a transmission medium.

Baseband. In analog terms, the original bandwidth of a signal from a device. Also used in digital transmission to describe some local area networks. In analog terms, the original bandwidth of a signal from a device (e.g., 3 kHz for telephone, 4.5 mHz for television). Also used in digital transmission to describe some local area networks. In modulation, where the ratio of the upper to the lower limit of the frequency band is large compared to the unity of transmitted signals.

Baseband Signaling System. A way of transmitting data on a local area network using:
- Coaxial cable or twisted-pair wire.
- Digital signals.
- Inexpensive transcievers.
- Distributed control.

Bell Operating Companies (BOCs). The 22 local operating companies divested from AT&T in 1984 and reorganized into seven regional holding or operating companies. After divestiture, these companies are allowed to provide only services and no hardware or terminal equipment.

Bidirectional. Ability to transfer data in either direction. This is characteristic of a bus local area network.

Binary. The fundamental number system used with computers. Binary numbers are represented by only two numerals, 0 and 1. The binary system is necessary because electrical circuits store and sense only two states: ON and OFF.

Binary Code. A code which is based on only two characters, 0 and 1.

Bi-Synchronous. Binary and synchronous signaling.

BISYNC (Binary Synchronous Communication). A method of transmission normally used by IBM mainframes. BISYNC gathers together a number of message characters and puts them in a single large message block that includes special characters, synchronized bits, and station addressing information.

Bit (Binary Digit). A unit of information that designates one of two possible values. A bit is usually written as a 1 or 0 to represent the ON or OFF status of an electrical switch. A bit is the smallest entity of a memory word in which a value can be stored. A computer term denoting the smallest logical piece of information. The smallest entity of a memory word in which a value can be stored.

Bridge. Equipment that allows interconnection of LANs, permitting communications between devices on separate networks using similar protocols.

Bridging. A term used to describe the linking of three or more communications lines, usually via telephone circuits as in a multipoint conference call.

Broadband. Communications that take advantage of a transmission medium known as frequency division multiplexing (FDM) to divide a single channel into a number of smaller, independent-frequency channels. The resultant wide bandwidth allows more bits per unit of time to be moved from point to point and can be used to transfer voice, data, and video.

Broadband Channel. A communications channel with a large bandwidth or capacity. Very often, any channel wider than voice grade is considered to be a broadband channel.

Bulletin Board. An electronic file within an electronic mail or teleconferencing system. All participants can place public messages there.

Bus. A topology for local area networks that functions like a single line shared by a number of nodes. A group of parallel electrical connections that carry signals between computer components or devices within a local area network.

Bypass. The use of various communications technologies (microwave, satellite, fiber optics, cellular) to bypass the local telephone company's twisted-pair cable network.

CAI—Computer Aided Instructions.

CBMS—Computer Based Message System. Receives, stores, and transmits messages. Messages are delivered to electronic mailboxes assigned to each user.

CCITT—Consultative Committee for International Telephony and Telegraphy. A part of the International Telecommunications Union that sets standards for the world.

CRT Display. The television monitor usually associated with a computer terminal which displays text, graphic, and visual information.

Cable. A group of conductive elements, such as wires, or other media, such as fiber optics, packaged as a single line to interconnect communications systems.

Cable Television. A television system that uses a coaxial cable (a cable with a single wire at the center surrounded by an insulator and then another solid or woven copper conductor) to transmit or distribute the TV signal.

Calendar. A calendar is a permanent storage area associated with a group. It is used to contain information about appointments, business trips, meetings, vacation times, etc., for each member of a conference group.

Cathode-Ray Tube (CRT). A vacuum tube that generates and guides electrons onto a fluorescent screen to produce characters or graphic displays on video display screens.

Carrier. A provider of transmission capabilities available to the general public, sometimes referred to as a *common carrier* or *regulated carrier,* as it is regulated by the Federal Communications Commission (FCC) or state commissions.

Cellular Mobile Radio. A new concept in mobile telephone communications. In a cellular mobile communications system, a geographic area is divided into a number of adjacent cells. Each cell in the system contains a low-powered transmitter that covers that cell only. A central computer monitors the signal strength in each cell and switches it from one cell to the next.

Central Processing Unit (CPU). Electronic components that cause processing in a computer to occur by interpreting instructions, performing calculations, moving data in main computer storage, and controlling the input/output operations. A CPU consists of the arithmetic/logic unit and the control unit.

CENTREX. Service providing a business customer with direct inward dialing to its phone extension and direct outward dialing from them.

Central Office (CO) CENTREX switching equipment is provided in the central office, while CU-CENTREX is on the customer's premises.

Channel. A band of frequencies allocated for communications.

Character. A single printable letter (A–Z), numeral (0–9), or symbol (,%$.) used to represent data. Text symbols such as a space, tab, or carriage return are not visible as characters.

Character Code. Numerical values assigned to characters. The ASCII code is an example.

Circuit. A communications path between two points. A system of semiconductors and related electrical elements through which electrical current flows. In data communications, the electrical path providing one-way or two-way communication between two points.

Circuit Switching. Physical connection taking place between channels.

Coaxial Cable. Cable that has one insulated wire at the center. A second wire surrounds the insulation and is also insulated. A physical network medium that offers large bandwidth and the ability to support high data rates, with high immunity to electrical interference and a low incidence of errors.

CODEC. A chip in a telephone that can convert an analog signal to a digital pulse, or the reverse. An electronic device which converts analog signals to digital form and vice versa. CODEC stands for COder/DE-Coder. A codec is generally made up of a central processing unit (CPU) and memory.

Collision Detection (CD). The ability of a transmitting node to detect simultaneous transmission attempts on a shared medium.

Common Carrier. An organization (such as a telephone operating company) that provides communication services to the general public at nondiscriminatory rates, without control of message content. Such an entity is regulated by a state or federal agency.

Communicating Word Processors. Word processors that can transmit and receive document information between one another through the use of telephone channels.

Communications Satellite. A satellite used to receive and retransmit data, including video and audio signals. Communications satellites must be in a geostationary (stationary relative to the earth) or geosynchronous orbit located 22,300 miles above the equator.

Compatibility. (1) The potential of an instruction, program, or component to be used on more than one computer. (2) The ability of computers to work with other computers that are not necessarily similar in design or capabilities.

Computer. A programmable electric machine made up of a microprocessor, memory, keyboard, and monitor. It performs high-speed operations, using prewritten instructions.

Computer Architecture. Internal computer design based on the types of programs that will run on it and the number that can be run at one time.

Computer Graphics. Images generated as a result of interaction between a computer and its user. This ranges from simple token selection and display, to manipulation of tokens, to generation of images using an interactive programming language.

Computer Network. An interconnection of computer systems, terminals, and communications facilities.

Computer Teleconferencing. Interactive group communication in which a computer is used to receive, hold, and distribute messages among participants. Generally referred to as *store and mail.* In addition, the conferencing participants communicate using keyboards to transmit written messages to one another. Communication may be synchronous (interactive in real time), but is commonly asynchronous (messages are stored in a central computer until retrieved by their intended recipients).

Computer Terminal. A typewriter-like device that can be connected to a computer for the input and output of data.

Configuration. The assortment of equipment (disks, diskettes, terminals, printers, etc.) in a particular system.

Contention. A conflict between two or more devices trying simultaneously to access a common channel.

Customer Premises Equipment (CPE). Terminal equipment, supplied by either the telephone common carrier or by a competitive supplier, which is connected to the telephone network.

Data. Information in the form of facts, numbers, letters, and symbols that can be stored in a computer. For personal computer users, data can be thought of as the basic elements of information created or processed by an application program.

Data Bank. A collection of data stored on auxiliary storage devices.

Database. A large collection of organized data that is required for performing a task. Typical examples are personnel files or stock quotations. An organized set of data accessible by a computer program for purposes of updating, deleting, and reporting.

Database Management Software. A system of integrated tools to store, retrieve, and maintain a large collection of data. Some of the tools support functions like batch reporting, interactive query, and decision support.

Data Code. A binary representation of a letter or number used by particular equipment.

Data Communication. The movement of coded data from a sender to a receiver by means of electrically transmitted signals.

Data Processing. The application in which a computer works primarily with numerical data, as opposed to text. Many computers can perform data and word processing. The catch-all term for all facets of computing. More precisely, data processing involves the use of computers for the manipulation of large quantities of data, with relatively low emphasis on calculation.

Data Set. (1) Another name for a modem. (2) A group of data elements.

Decentralized Processing. An arrangement of computers at remote locations communicating with a central processing unit, but not communicating directly with each other.

Dedicated. Committed to one specific use, such as a dedicated port on a computer to a specified terminal or microcomputer.

Dedicated Computer. A computer built for one special function, such as controlling the Space Shuttle's navigation system.

Degradation. Deterioration in the quality or speed of data transmission, caused as more users access a computer or computer network.

Digital. A method of representing information using a sequence of ones and zeros for storage and interpretation by a computer. In digital transmission analog signals, which are originally in a continuous form, are converted to discrete signals of zeros or ones to be transmitted to a receive site, interpreted, and used to reconstruct the original analog signal.

Digital Signal. A series of electrical impulses that carry information in computer circuits.

Digitize. To translate voice or pictorial signals into binary code (digital format) for transmission.

Direct Connect Modem. A modem that plugs directly into a telephone outlet, bypassing the handset. It enables users to send and receive signals directly to and from telephone lines. See *Acoustic Coupler.*

Direct Distance Dialing (DDD). The accessing of telephones tied to the public-switched network through the use of an area code (NPA), an exchange, and a local telephone number. DDD, which is the same as message telecommunications service (MTS), differs from WATS in that with DDD the user receives an itemized accounting of each call, whereas with WATS there is no accounting.

Directory. An index used by a control program to locate blocks of data that are stored in separate areas of a data set in direct access storage.

Disk. A flat, circular plate with a magnetic coating for storing data. Physical size and storage capacity of disks can vary. There are hard disks and diskettes, also called floppy disks, and optical disks.

Disk Drive. The machine that contains the disk pack. The disk drive has read/write heads that can deposit data on the disk and retrieve data from it.

Diskette. A flexible, flat, circular plate that is permanently housed in a black paper envelope. It stores data and software on its magnetic coating. Standard sizes are 5.25 inches and 8 inches in diameter. Diskettes are often called *floppy disks*.

Display Screen. A device that provides a visual representation of data; a TV-like screen often called a monitor.

Distributed Data Processing. A computing approach in which an organization uses computers in more than one location, rather than one large computer in a single location.

Distribution List. A list that identifies a collection of members. The name of the distribution list serves as shorthand in addressing groups collectively.

Document Transmission. The electronic transmission of information shown on the surface of a flat document. Often referred to as facsimile, as the original document stays in one location while a facsimile of that document is printed at the receive sites. Also includes high-speed document scanners which are used in video conferencing rooms.

Download. The process of loading software into the nodes of a network from one node or device over the network media.

Dumb Terminal. A terminal that consists of a keyboard and an output device such as a printer or a screen. A dumb terminal is used for simple input/output operations. It has no intelligence of its own and is not capable of processing information.

Earth Station. Ground-based equipment used to communicate with satellites.

Electronic Blackboard. This is a generic name used for large table audiographic devices. It is a system for sending writing over a normal telephone line. As the sender writes on a normal-looking chalkboard, the writing appears at the distant location on a television monitor.

Electronic Circuit. A pathway or channel through which electricity flows.

Electronic File Cabinet. An electronic storage unit that files data in much the same way as a regular file cabinet. It has some distinct advantages: a great deal of information can be stored in a small area, accessed and changed quickly, organized more efficiently, and kept more securely.

Electronic Handshake. An arrangement where sending equipment can electronically query receiving equipment regarding transmitting speeds, more selection, line quality, and other conditions for the most compatible transmitting conditions.

Electronic Mail. A system by which written messages are entered through a keyboard and distributed to individuals or groups subscribing to the service. Messages are generally stored on a computer and forwarded to recipients when they request messages through the use of a data terminal or other keyboard device.

Ergonomics. The scientific study and planning of the workplace in order to adapt it to the mental and physical needs of the worker. One of the office-design industry's buzz words.

Exchange, Private Automatic (PAX). A dial telephone exchange that provides private telephone service to an organization and that does not allow calls to be transmitted to or from the public telephone network.

Exchange, Private Branch (PBX). A private automatic telephone exchange that provides for the transmission of calls internally and to and from the public telephone network.

Face to Face. The generally accepted meeting format where all parties are physically in the same place at the same time.

Facsimile (Fax). A device that electronically transmits information written or printed on paper. The text or graphic material is scanned, and the image is converted to signals. These are transmitted by telephone to a compatible terminal which is able to produce a copy. Generally used to convey images of typewritten forms, printed figures, or hand-drawn diagrams to other sites participating in a teleconference. At the receive site, the image is reproduced on a sheet of paper. Images transmitted are high-contrast monochrome. Facsimile devices are commonly referred to as fax, telecopiers, or datafax.

Fiber-Optic Waveguides. Thin filaments of glass or other transparent materials through which a light beam can be transmitted for long distances by means of multiple internal reflections.

File. One or more records of information stored as a unit. A collection of logically related records or data. A file is the means by which data is stored on a disk or diskette so it can be used at a later time.

Filename. The sequence of alphanumeric characters assigned by a user so a file can be read by the computer and the user.

Flat Rate. A fixed payment for service, independent of use, within a defined area, with an additional charge for each call outside the area.

Flow Control. A process of developing the orderly flow of data traffic across a data communications channel.

Freeze-Frame Transmission. Transmission of high-quality, still-motion images, about one each 13 seconds. It is used in slow-scan teleconferencing.

Frequency Division Multiplex (FDM). A modulation technique that divides the total capacity of a communication media into channels with each channel assigned a specific frequency band.

Frequency Division Multiple Access (FDMA). An access method to a common channel by a population of communicating devices that allocates a portion of the capacity of the channel on a pair-by-pair basis using frequency division multiplexing (FDM).

Full-Motion Video. Provides interactive group communications through the use of continuous motion television images though not necessarily broadcast quality (6 megaHz). Some systems operate at 3 megaHz, 1.544 megabits per second, or less.

Gateway. A special node that interfaces two or more dissimilar networks, providing protocol translation between the networks.

Graphics. The use of lines and figures to display data, as opposed to the use of printed characters.

HDLC—High-Level Data Link Control. A bit-oriented protocol designated by ISO, originally developed by IBM.

Hard Copy. Data or information printed on paper copy.

Hardware. Components of a computer system that have a physical substance as opposed to software.

Hardwired. A permanent physical connection between two points in an electrical circuit or between two devices linked by a communication line. Personal computer local connections are typically hardwired. In contrast, all connectors through a modem are switched (turned on and off) because they use telephone lines.

Hertz. Named after Heinrich Rudolph Hertz, a German physicist. A measure of frequency, one cycle or complete oscillation of a radio waveform per second. A unit of frequency equal to one cycle per second (CPS). 1 kHz = 1,000 CPS, 1 mHz = 1 megahertz or 1,000,000 CPS.

Host Computer. The primary or controlling computer in a multiple-computer operation on which the smaller computers depend to do most work.

ISO—International Standards Organization.

Information Management. Evaluation and modeling tools that use the information stored in a well-structured data collection.

Information Resource Management (IRM). A term generally used to describe an organizational structure and a high-tech approach to managing new technology.

Information Services. Publicly accessible computer repositories for data, such as stock exchange prices or foreign currency exchange rate, and other databases.

INPUT-OUTPUT (I/O) Device. A system component used to transfer data between the main storage and other devices such as the CPU, terminals, or printers.

Installation. The process of putting a computer system, hardware and software, into a location; connecting the hardware for use; and loading the software onto the computer.

Intelligent Terminal. A terminal that is capable of processing information; many store and retrieve information on their own tapes, disks, and printers. An intelligent terminal can be adapted to communicate with various host computers simply by changing the protocol programmed into it.

Intelsat—The International Telecommunications Satellite Consortium. Formed in 1964 with the purpose of creating a worldwide communications satellite system.

Interactive. Capable of carrying on a dialogue with the user, through a keyboard, rather than simply responding to commands.

Interactive Software Package. A program that provides the user with commands with which to submit requests and exercise control over the execution of the program.

Interconnect Company. An organization that supplies telephone equipment by sale, rental, or leasing, other than the serving telephone company.

Interface. (1) A component that acts as a translator between circuits and other components of a system or other systems. A hardware connection that provides an electronic pathway for signals, or software that enables information to be exchanged between programs. Keyboards interface people and processors. (2) A common boundary—for example, the connection point between two subsystems or devices. The interconnection between business machines and the data set, modem, or communications channel.

International Record Carriers. Carriers (FTC Communications, ITT, RCA, TRT, and Western Union) which provide voice, data, and other transmission services such as telex, facsimile, etc., between the U.S. and a foreign country.

Key Systems. A key system is the central unit that is used when more than one telephone line per set is required. It can switch individual telephones to a limited number of trunks. It offers flexibility and a wide variety of uses, i.e. pickup of several central-office lines, foreign exchange lines, and PBX stations lines.

LAN—Local Area Network. A communications network connecting computer terminals and other devices within an organization. LANs may also connect with other private or public networks.

Leased Line. A permanent telephone circuit used for transmitting voice or data signals. The line is leased from a long-distance telephone company (common carrier) such as AT&T, and can be conditioned to permit higher transmission speeds than a standard line (see *Voice Grade Line*).

Light Pen. A device that allows data to be entered or altered on a CRT screen.

Line Printer. A device that prints, at high speed, hard-copy data information that is outputted by a computer.

MTS—Message Telecommunications Service. An FCC term for long-distance telephone calling.

Magnetic Tape (Magtape). Tape used as a mass storage media and packaged on reels. Since the data stored on magnetic tape can only be accessed serially, it is not practical for use with personal computers. It is often used as a backup device on larger computer systems.

Mail Qualifier. An attribute of information. Examples are:
- Recipient.
- Sender.
- Forwarding permission.
- Copy permission.
- Special mailcode.
- Request for response.
- Site ID.
- Modification capability.
- Keep capability.

Mainframe. Centralized computer facility (CPU and main memory). It may delegate some of its workload to specialized processors.

Mass Storage. A device such as a disk or magtape that can store large amounts of data readily accessible to the central processing unit.

Matrix Management. An arrangement where work is organized around organizational work groups.

Meet Me. A term used to describe a dial-up audio conferencing system. All members of the conference dial the same number and are bridged together.

Menu. A list of choices available to a user that is presented on a monitor. The user selects an action to be performed by typing a letter or by positioning the cursor.

Menu-Driven. A computer system that primarily uses menus rather than a command language for its directions.

Message Switching. Routing data toward its destination. This is done by the computer processor.

Microcomputer. A computer that uses a microprocessor chip (integrated circuit) as its central processing unit. A small computer that has all the hardware components of a large computer but in smaller sizes. Sometimes called a personal computer (PC) or small business computer. They usually support one user, but with increased power may provide processing for several terminals. They are physically very small and can fit on or under a desk. Microcomputer technology is based on larger-scale integration (LSI) circuitry. Micros are usually the least expensive of the computer types.

Microprocessor. An integrated circuit using semiconductor technology, which incorporates all the elements for performing arithmetic operations and manipulating data.

Microwave. The electromagnetic transmission of audio, video, or data communications at high radio frequencies. A clear line of sight is required from transmitter to receiver.

Minicomputer. A small computer that has all the hardware components of a large computer but in smaller sizes. A minicomputer is usually slower in processing speed than a large computer.

Modems (MOdulator/DEModulator). A hardware device that permits computers and terminals to communicate with each other using analog circuits such as telephone lines. The modem's modulator translates the digital computer signals into analog signals that can be transmitted over a telephone line. The modem's demodulator converts analog signals into digital signals for the computer's use.

Modulation. The process of adding information in the form of an analog signal to an existing signal carried by a transmission medium. The added signal effectively "rides along" the transmission signal.

Monitor. A television-like display screen that can be used as an output device. It is also called display screen, cathode ray tube (CRT), and video display terminal (VDT).

Multiplexing. The use of a common physical channel to make two or more logical channels, either by splitting the frequency band transmitted by the common channel into narrower bands, each of which is used to constitute a distinct channel (frequency division multiplex), or by allotting this common channel in turn to constitute different, intermittent channels (time division multiplex).

Multiplexor (or Multiplexer). Equipment that permits simultaneous transmission of multiple signals over one physical circuit. A device that combines streams of information into a composite signal and sends them along a communicating channel. A similar device reverses the process at the receiving end of a transmission.

Multipoint. Refers to a line with more than two stations connected.

Multiprocessing. Processing by two or more computers connected to run jobs concurrently for faster results.

Multi-to-Single. Transmission of signals from a number of sites to a single location.

Narrowband Channel. Generally refers to a telephone circuit capable of handling 3000 Hz. A narrowband facility or normal telephone line, by definition, can handle a bandwidth of 20 kHz or less.

Network. An interconnected and coordinated system of geographically dispersed communications devices (terminals) so that signal transmission to or among any of the devices is practical and reliable. The computers can send and receive data among themselves and share certain devices such as hard disks and printers.

Network Management. Administrative services performed in managing a network, such as network topology and software configuration, downloading of software, monitoring network performance, maintaining network operations, and diagnosing and troubleshooting problems.

Node. A connecting point on a communicating network or between communicating channels.

Nonsimultaneous Communication. Messages being received and transmitted at a terminal while the operator is performing other functions.

OCC—Other Common Carrier. A term generally used to describe telephone service companies other than AT&T, but now including AT&T. See *SCC*.

OEM—Original Equipment Manufacturer. A term used to describe the manufacturer who created the product, regardless of whose name is on the product.

Off-Line. Not connected to a central computer; normally using a personal computer without being connected to a host mainframe computer or distance computer system.

On-Line. Equipment or information that is presently part of or connected to the operating computer system. Used commonly in computer teleconferencing to indicate that a site is active and that participants are able to receive and/or transmit during a teleconference.

Operating System. The basic system program that ensures orderly execution of all computer actions.

Optical Disk. Computer storage (memory) disk. They have potential for far greater capacity than magnetic disks. Some can be re-recorded.

Organizational Directory. A directory of a computer conferencing system that contains information relating to its members, centers, and groups.

Output. Information produced as a result of processing input data.

Owner. Creator of an electronic message or document.

PBX—Private Branch Exchange. Equipment originally used as a means of switching telephone calls within a business site and from the site to outside lines. The newest, third-generation PBXs are digital switches which handle both voice and data communications.

Packet. A set number of characters that can be switched and transmitted along a communication network in a specific format. A collection of bits that contain both control information and data. The basic unit of transmission in a packet-switched network. Control information is carried in the packet, along with the data, to provide for such functions as addressing, sequencing, flow control, and error control at each of several protocol levels. A packet can be of fixed or variable length, but generally has a specified length.

Packet Switching. A relatively new form of digital communication in which data bits are grouped into bursts (or packets) of fixed length so they can share a channel with other such bursts. When received at the destination, the bursts are separated and sent to the appropriate recipients.

Parameter. A range of characteristics of a program, record, or other area.

Password. A word each user may attach to his or her mailname. Passwords may also be attached to groups and centers.

Peripheral. A device that is external to the CPU and main memory, but connected to it. A printer, modem, or terminal would be an example.

Personal Computer. See *Microcomputer.*

Plotter. A graphic drawing device.

Point-to-Multipoint. A telecommunications configuration which allows information to be communicated from one point to many. In some point-to-multipoint teleconferencing systems, there are a single transmitting site and many receiving sites located independently of one another.

Point-to-Point. A telecommunications configuration which allows only two sites to communicate with one another. In most cases both sites can send as well as receive.

Polling. A continuous checking of device status. A method of controlling the transmission sequence by requiring each device on a multipoint line to wait until the controlling processor requests it to transmit.

Port. An input and/or output socket on a computer that is used to connect hardware such as modems or cables.

Power Supply. A transistor switch that converts AC power into DC power. It energizes components such as integrated circuits, monitors, and keyboards, and steps down the power supplied to some components.

Processor. The controlling unit or processing part of the computer system that reads, interprets, and executes instructions.

Program. The complete sequence of instructions and routines needed to solve a problem or to execute directions in a computer.

Programming Language. The words, mnemonics, and/or symbols, along with the specific rules allowed in constructing computer programs. Some examples are BASIC, FORTRAN, and COBOL.

Primary Station. The main station in a telecommunications network. In an SDLC environment, the main station is usually a front-end processor.

Printer. A device that prints data output from a computer in paper copy.

Printout. Any computer-generated hard copy.

Program. The complete sequence of instructions and routines needed to solve a problem or to execute directions in a computer.

Protocol. A set of rules and conventions that governs the orderly and meaningful exchange of information between or among communications parties. Hardware and software protocols can be defined.

Protocol Converter. A device for translating the data transmission code and/or protocol of one network or device to the corresponding code or protocol of another network or device, enabling equipment with different conventions to communicate with one another.

Public Data Network (PDN). A packet-switched or circuit-switched network that is available for use by many customers. A PDN may offer value-added services at a reduced cost because of communications resource sharing, and it will usually provide increased reliability due to built-in redundancy.

Real-Time. The actual time an event is occurring. A term used to describe an on-line interactive application. A computer conference can be held in real-time or asynchronously.

Record. A collection of related data items.

Regional Bell Operating Company (RBOC). One of the seven holding companies formed by the divestiture of AT&T to provide both regulated and nonregulated telephone services; includes Bell Atlantic, NYNEX, BellSouth, Pacific Telesis, U.S. West, Southwestern Bell Corp., and Ameritech.

Remote Terminal. Input/output equipment attached to a system through a transmission network.

Resale Carrier. A company which redistributes the services of another common carrier and retails the services to the public.

Resolution. This is the degree of detail that can be seen on a display screen.

Resource Directory. An electronic file containing information associated with all private and public permanent storage areas within a computer conference.

Ring. A network topology in which stations are connected to one another in a close, logical circle. Typically, access to the media passes sequentially from one station to the next by means of polling from a master station or by passing an access token from one station to another.

SCC—Specialized Common Carrier. A term used to describe long-distance suppliers other than Bell. See *OCC*.

Satellite Communications. Provides high-volume, long-distance transmission of signals that can be used for voice, video, and data communications. The satellites in orbit receive signals, amplify them, and broadcast them to all earth stations that are situated in the antenna pattern.

Serial Communication. Data transmission in which each bit is sent separately and sequentially.

Shared User. One who shares computer resources.

Shared-Tenant Services. Integrated telecommunications systems and related services provided for and shared by a building's tenants. Also referred to as *multitenant services.*

Signal Security. Scrambling of signal to block eavesdropping of teleconferences. Also known as *encryption.*

Simplex Communications. Allows movement in a single direction only.

Simulation. When one system imitates the actual behavior of another. The simulator will transmit and receive the same data and produce results identical to the results produced by the simulated device.

Single-line Installation. A PBX or key system directly connected to the telephone network, as opposed to an extension or key system located behind a PBX or CENTREX system.

Size. Usually refers to the amount of storage a system has available on-line; also refers to the number of words a memory contains and to the processing capacity of the CPU.

Slow-Scan Television. See Freeze-Frame Transmission.

Soft Copy. Information presented on a display screen or in audio format, rather than as printed copy.

Software. Custom or packaged, produced as either data, video, or audio cassette that contains information that can be presented or processed. Instructions that make a computer perform a specific task or program.

Software Interface. A program that controls the way a computer program interacts with other programs it uses.

Sort. Rearranging information that has been filed in *fields.*

Speakerphone. An amplified telephone, allowing hands-free usage.

Speed Dialing. A device that can be programmed to automatically dial telephone calls by simply dialing a single or double digit. Station speed dialing is accomplished at the telephone set, whereas system-wide speed dialing is provided by the PBX or telephone equipment.

Standard Member. A standard member in a computer conference is a participation in the system without specific role.

Star. A network topology consisting of one central node with point-to-point links to several other nodes. Control of the network is usually located in the central node or switch, with all routing of network message traffic performed by the central node.

Star Network. A network containing a central computer at the hub. All equipment radiates from that center.

Station Message Detail Recording (SMDR). Provides a record of the calling station or attendant number, starting time, call duration, all digits of the called number, and the specific trunk or trunk group used for outgoing calls. Different manufacturers take various approaches to providing this total service, and may or may not include a terminal device for printouts or a processing service to manipulate the recorded data in order to produce a variety of management reports and summaries. In almost all cases, this data is accumulated on magnetic tape or similar storage medium; however, a few systems bypass any storage steps and provide a line printer for a written record of outgoing calls as they occur.

Still Frame. A slow-scan video image, as in a slide show.

Storage. Also called data storage. Usually refers to disk packs and/or magnetic tapes.

Storage Media Capacity. Maximum number of characters the storage media such as mag cards, disks, or tapes can hold.

Storage Media Standard. The design of disks and tapes used to store memory.

String. Alphanumeric data treated as a unit.

Subscriber. A system using the services of a network, such as an S.25 network.

Switched Line. A type of data-communications line used to connect computers over a regular telephone network.

Switched Network. A network that allows any site connected to it to communicate with any other site connected to the same network. The public toll telephone network or message telecommunications system (MTS) is referred to as the *public switched telephone network* (PSTN).

Synchronous Transssmission. A method of high-speed transmission in which the timing of each bit of data is precisely controlled. Communications in which there is a constant time between successive bits, characters, or events. The timing is achieved by synchronizing the clocking of data transmission.

System. Refers to an entire PBX or CENTREX installation, including all individual telephone instruments, wire, cable, and common equipment.

System Center. A center established during the initiation phase of the system and will exist during its lifetime.

System Components. The physical parts of a system, such as a keyboard, CRT display, minicomputer, mag-card reader or floppy-disk drive, and printing device.

System Security. Some systems provide an electronic key lock to prevent unauthorized access. A few systems have security codes so that only certain persons may have access to any stored document. This can be valuable if documents are being processed which should have restricted staff access.

T-1 Carrier. A method of multiplexing or combining 24 voice signals together for long-distance transmission purposes. The speed of this U.S. digital transmission is 1,544,000 bits per second. Using T-1 can reduce long-distance carrier charges and provide end-to-end digital transmission.

Tap. A device in the feeder cable that connects a device to a network.

Telecommunications. Communications over distance using electronic means; types of telecommunications channels include twisted-pair telephone lines, coaxial cable, microwave, satellite, and fiber-optic cable.

Teleconferencing. The use of telecommunications systems by groups of three or more people, at two or more locations, for the purpose of conferring with one another. Also the two-way communication between two or more groups, or three or more individuals remote from each other, using a telecommunications medium. Also the interactive group communication through an electronic medium.

Terminal. Any device capable of sending and/or receiving information over a communications channel.

Tieline (Tie Trunk). A trunk between two PBXs which permits extensions in one PBX to be connected to extensions on the other PBX.

Time Division Multiple Access (TDMA). An accessing technique which allows separate communications sources to share the same telecommunications channel. Each user site has a time slot allocated during which data for that site may be transmitted or received.

Time Division Multiplexing (TDM). A method of using channel capacity efficiently, in which each node is allotted a small time interval, in turns, during which it may transmit a message or portion of a message. Nodes are given unique time slots during which they have exclusive command of the channel. The messages of many channels are interleaved for transmission and then de-multiplexed into their proper order at the receiving end.

Time-Shared Computer. A computer system which provides multiuser access at a rapid rate under control of the computer operating system.

Token Bus. A token access procedure used with broadbase topology or network.

Token Passing. A method whereby each device on a local area network receives and passes the right to use the channel. Tokens are special bit patterns or packets, usually several bits in length, which circulate from node to node when there is no message traffic. Possession of the token gives exclusive access to the network for message transmission.

Token Ring. The token access procedure used on a network with a sequential or ring topology.

Topology. Network topology can be centralized or distributed. Centralized networks, or star-like networks, have all nodes connected to a single node. Alternative topology is distributed; that is, in the limit, each node is connected to every other node. Typical topology names include bus, ring, and star.

Traffic. The measurement of data movement, volume, and velocity over a communications link.

Transmission Line. The means by which a signal is sent and received.

Transportable Earth Station. A fully mobile unit capable of sending and receiving to and from a satellite.

Two-Way Audio; One-Way Live Video. A teleconference in which the audience at multiple sites receives a transmission from a central point of origin and participates through a telephone or video conference system.

Two-Wire Circuit. Typically a telephone circuit between a central office and a customer's premises which takes both the send and receive signals on a single pair of wires. Between central offices on the toll network, four wires are used, two for transmission and two for receipt.

Uploading. Shifting information from memory banks of one computer to another.

User Interface. The pathway or connection between a person and device.

Value-Added Carriers. A communications network that provides additional services.

Value-Added Network. Additional applications/services, such as packet switching, protocol conversion, public dial access, error control communications, etc., which add value to the conventional data communications network.

Vendor Independence. The ability to allow devices manufactured by different vendors, often using different protocols, to communicate with each other.

Vertical Scrolling. Vertical movement of characters on a display screen that allows more lines to be shown.

Videotex. A service that uses a part or all of a TV screen for information displays called pages or frames. The information could range from weather or news to advertising for various services.

Virtual Circuit. Logical connection of communicating devices for duration of the transmission.

Voice Grade Line. A normal telephone line designed for voice communication. It can be used for data transmission rates of up to 1200 baud. A communications circuit which generally delivers 3–4 kHz of analog bandwidth. Typically used for telephone conversations or graphic or data communications devices requiring narrowband circuits.

Voice Mail. A system that provides computer-controlled deposit, storage, and delivery of voice messages.

Wide Area Network. Earth stations where signals are digitized, multiplexed, and sent via satellite to other earth stations. Used in long-distance transmission.

Wide Area Telecommunications Service (WATS). An offering by AT&T Communications whereby a discount rate is offered on long-distance charges to users for not receiving the billing of each telephone call.

Wideband. Typically used to describe a signal which has a bandwidth of 20 kHz or greater. When used in describing switches, typically implies a system capable of switching circuits at 4 kHz or higher.

Word Processor. A dedicated device, or a software package on a computer, which allows sophisticated text editing of documents stored on an electronic medium, such as a floppy disk.

Workstation. A location at which an individual works; generally used to denote electronic, usually computer-linked, devices which an individual uses in the course of his or her job, in an automated office setting.

X.25. A CCITT standard that defines the interface between a public display network (PDN) and a packet-mode user device (DTE). It also defines the services that these devices can expect from the X.25 PDN, including the ability to establish virtual circuits through a PDN to another user device, to move data from one user device to another, and to destroy the virtual circuit when through.

NOTES _____

Chapter Two

[1] John Naisbitt, *Megatrends* (New York: Warner Books, 1982), p. 11.

[2] John Naisbitt, *Megatrends* (New York: Warner Books, 1982), p. 1

[3] *IBIS Executive Report*, Cross Information Company, November 1984, p. 253.

[4] "Telecommunications Seen as Offering New Opportunities for Increased Productivity," *Communications News* (December 1984), p. 97.

[5] Arthur Rubin, "The Automated Office: An Environment for Productive Work, or an Information Factory?," *Executive Summary* (Center for Building Technology/National Engineering Laboratory/National Bureau of Standards, November 1983), p. 3. The study Rubin draws from is entitled "White Collar Productivity: The National Challenge," done by The Productivity Center, Houston, Texas, 1983.

[6] Daniel Golman, "The Electronic Rorschach," *Psychology Today*, February 1983, p. 39. A study of 15 corporations conducted by the consulting firm of Booz, Allen, and Hamilton.

[7] James H. Green, *Automating Your Office*, (New York: McGraw-Hill, 1984), p. 3.

[8] John Daly, corporate telecommunications manager for the Planning & Research Corp, an engineering and professional services firm headquartered in McLean, Va. Speech at Intelligent Buildings & Information Systems Conference, Sept. 1984, Cross Information Company, Boulder, CO.

[9] "Profit-Making Pros and Cons Are Involved in Telecommunications Resale and Tenant Services," *Communications News*, November 1984, p. 90.

[10] "Growing Multi-Tenant Services Trend Spreads Access to Latest Technology," *Communications News* (November 1984), p. 32.

[11] John Naisbitt, *Megatrends*, (New York: Warner Books, 1982), p. 1.

[12] Arthur Rubin, "The Automated Office," p. 3.

[13] Cross Information Company, Intelligent Buildings and Information Systems Conference, September 1984.

[14] Lois Friedland, "Where High Tech and Humans Meet," (February 1985), p. 53.

[15] "Profit-Making Pros and Cons Are Involved in Telecommunications Resale and Tenant Services," *Communications News*, (November, 1984), p. 90.

[16] Charlie Blaine, "Intelligent Buildings," *USA Today*, August 1, 1984, p. 1B.

[17] "The Word on Smart Buildings," *Teleconnect*, November 1984, p. 98.

[18] Joe Baker, "How to be a Shared Tenant Provider," *Teleconnect*, (November 1984), p. 89. Joe Baker is the national marketing manager of multi-tenant services for Northern Telecom.

[19] *IBIS Executive Report*, (Cross Information Company, November 1984, p. 7.

[20] Bruce W. Most, "Smart Buildings," *American Way*, October 1984, p. 162.

Chapter Three

[1] Office Automation Conference Digest, February 4–6, 1985, Atlanta, Georgia, p. 62.

[2] Kathleen Kelleher and Thomas B. Cross, *Teleconferencing: Linking People Together Electronically*, (Englewood Cliffs, N.J.: Prentice-Hall, 1985), pp. 209–210.

Chapter Four

[1] Larry Stockett, Untitled working paper, March 1985, p. 21.

[2] "Cable Television Comes of Age," *Communications News* September, 1984, p. 92.

[3] John E. Martin, interview by editor Paul Finney, "The Encryption Option: Using a Key to Unscramble Confidential Messages," *Management Technology* (October 1984), p. 58.

[4] William A. Demers, "Records Management: The Coming Transformation," *Today's Office* (October 1984), p. 71.

[5] William A. Demers, "Records Management: The Coming Transformation," *Today's Office* (October 1984), p. 71. [according to Donald Newman, program manager of the File Management Systems section of 3M's Office Systems Division.] PA

[6] William A. Demers, "Records Management: The Coming Transformation," *Today's Office* (October 1984), p. 71.

[7] *Infosystems* (June 1984), p. 7.

Chapter Six

[1] Alex Hicks, "Energy . . . need to upgrade just to hold the line on costs," *Business Facilities* (October 1984), p. 50.

Chapter Seven

[1] Gordon J. Lorig, Jr., "Communications as a Resource Within the Intelligent Building," *Office Automation Conference* Georgia World Congress Center, Atlanta, February 4–6, 1985.

[2] AT&T has recently been developing software for central office 1A ESS switches which will allow for SMDR. In addition, software for message center services, facilities management, CENTREX station arrangement, and automatic call-distribution support are part of the six-part Advanced Communications Package which started regular shipment as of January 11, 1985. *Communications Week*, Monday, February 11, 1985, p. 39.

[3] Interview with Rudolpho X. Munguia, March 21, 1985.

[4] James L. Coggins, "Telecontrolling Energy Through Local Area Networks," *BOMA International Skylines* (September 1984), pp. 20–21.

[5] Ibid., pp. 20–21.

Chapter Eight

[1] Francis Duffy, "Offices: Escape from the Banal," *The Architectural Review* (November 1983), p. 34.

[2] Arthur Rubin, "The Automated Office: An Environment for Productive Work, or an Information Factory?" *Executive Summary*, (Center for Building Technology/National Engineering Laboratory/National Bureau of Standards, November 1983).

[3] "Interim Design Guidelines for Automated Offices," Center for Building Technology, (NBSIR 84–2908, August 1984), pp. 53–54.

[4] Susan J. Biagiotti with William F. Ablondi, "Micros by the Millions: Future Computing Sizes Up the Desktop User Scene," *Management Technology* (December 1984), p. 58.

[5] Arthur Andersen & Co. "Trends in Information Technology," *Teleconnect*, January 1985, p. 127.

[6] Don Korrel, Interview of Don Korrel by Thomas B. Cross, January 1985.

[7] NOPA Study Report: "Design is Vital to Productivity Drives," *Facilities Design and Management* January 1984, p. 14.

[8] Arthur Rubin, "The Automated Office," p. 3.

[9] "Study: 10% of workers use VDTs," *Daily Camera*, Nov. 19, 1984, p. 7.

[10] Walter B. Kleeman, Jr., "The Electronic Office-Design Opportunity," *Electronic Office Design*, May 1984, p. 8.

[11] "Rapid Electronic Development Shapes 'Office of Future' Design," *Contract* (January 1985), p. 189.

[12] Arthur Rubin, "The Automated Office," p. 10.

[13] Lois Friedland, "Where High Tech and Humans Meet," *Sky* (February 1985), p. 53.

[14] R. Marans and K. Spreckelmeyer, "Evaluating Open and Conventional Office Design," *Environment and Behavior* 14, no. 3 May 1982.

[15] Arthur Rubin, "The Automated Office," pp. 10–11.

[16] Don Korell, "Planning for the Future Office—Today," director of research, Steelcase Inc., unpublished paper, p. 7.

[17] Stephanie K. Walker, "The Computerized Office: Using Flexible Furniture to Boost Productivity," *Management Technology* (September 1984), p. 27.

[18] Walter B. Kleeman, Jr., "The Electronic Office-Design," p. 8.

[19] *Video Display, Work and Viscon* (Washington, D.C.: National Academy Press, 1980).

[20] Arthur Rubin, "The Automated Office," p. 10.

[21] Francis Duffy (Principal author), *The ORBIT Study: Information Technology and Office Design*, April 1983, p. 54.

[22] Philip J. Stone and Robert Luchetti, "Your Office is Where You Are," *Harvard Business Review* March–April 1985, p. 103.

Chapter Nine

[1] Leeza L. Hoyt, "Preparing for the Office of the Future," *Journal of Property Management* (March–April 1985), p. 10. The study, entitled "Office '88: In Search of Office Excellence," is an 11-part study which took an in-depth look at the office of the future. Members of the research team included one of the largest contract furniture dealerships in southern California, Interior Resources; Walker Associates, Inc., interior architects; Gensler Associates, architects; and BOSTI (Buffalo Organization for Social and Technological Innovation).

[2] Arthur Rubin, "The Automated Office: An Environment for Productive Work, or an Information Factory?" *Executive Summary*" (Center for Building Technology/National Engineering Laboratory/National Bureau of Standards, November 1983), p. 7.

[3] Facilities, Newsletter Budstrode Press, London, England, (November 1984), p. 2. In 1968, office floor space use broke down as 84 percent for staff, 9 percent for equipment, and 7 percent for storage. Now 54 percent of the floor space is for staff, 32 percent for equipment, and 14 percent for storage.

[4] Arthur Rubin, "The Automated Office," p. 7.

[5] ORBIT Study, p. 1.

[6] Prof. Rigomar Thurmen, phone interview March 21, 1985.

[7] Leeza L. Hoyt, "Preparing for the Office of the Future," *Journal of Property Management*, (March—April 1985), p. 10.

[8] ORBIT Study, p. 72.

[9] Ibid, p. 102.